DAILY MANNA

(FOOD FOR THE HUNGRY SOUL)

…And Moses said unto them, this is the bread which the Lord hath given you to eat.

Exodus 16:15

Bishop Ronnie Whittier, Th.D.

Daily Manna (Food for the Hungry Soul) by Bishop Ronnie Whittier

Book Cover Design by Lady Lajuana Fields of Fields Creative Photography.

Scripture quotations taken from the King James Version (KJV) – public domain

ISBN: 978-0-578-46779-5

Printed in the United States of America

Dedication

I dedicate this book to my father, Bishop James A Whittier Sr., whom our Heavenly Father called home on May 10, 1998, and my loving mother, Queen E. Whittier, whom God has blessed me to yet enjoy her presence on this side of heaven. She has remained very faithful and supportive in her commitment to the ministry.

To my beloved wife, Evangelist Winnetta L. Whittier for her undaunted support. She has been an inspiration to me throughout our marriage and to my ministry to the Lord.

To my very talented loving daughters, Keisha, Alexis, and Rhonda for just being there always encouraging me. To my siblings to whom I'm happy to have many joyful experiences as they have always been a very big part of my life. I love every one of you.

To my beloved brother, Deacon Clifford M. Whittier, who finished his course in this life on April 12, 2006.

To my Emmanuel Temple Church Family that has encouraged me to go beyond the four walls of any building to share the unadulterated gospel of Jesus Christ.

A special thanks to Evangelist Mildred L. Buchanan, for her efforts of love prompting me to complete this long overdue work.

I also thank Evangelist Stacey L. Fields for her commitment to helping me to complete this work.

I'm excited and enthusiastic about the Living Word of God. I will read it, I will study it, I will live it and with God's help, I will share it.

Bishop Ronnie Whittier, Th.D.

TABLE of CONTENTS

Introduction

The purpose and vision of this book is to inspire Christians everywhere to grow toward spiritual maturity. The ultimate goal is for them to develop an acquired taste for Manna. The word "Manna" is found in the book of **Exodus 16:15** and means divinely supplied spiritual nourishment.

The difficulty that many Twenty-First Century Christians face is the inability to grow spiritually. This is an age old problem strongly engrafted in the very nature of man. We want the anointing without the trials. We want the wisdom without the test of time. We want success without the prerequisites required by God to be effective in our walk.

Spiritual Growth is as much a part of life as is breathing. We don't stop breathing to keep living life. Neither should we stop growing spiritually to better live this life. Spiritual Maturity is coming to the understanding that life has many turns with ups and downs. Having grown to this point creates a hunger and thirst to dine everyday in God's Café known as the Bible. You begin to anticipate a daily feeding of *Manna* that always feed your soul and enrich your life. As was evident in the life of Christ; He increased in wisdom, in stature, and in favor with God and man. **(St. Luke 2:52)**

Daily Manna builds your relationship with God, affords you strength to deal with life issues and awakens your sense of awareness to share your faith.

Dr. Ronnie Whittier, Th.D.

Foreword

It is indeed an honor to be able to write the foreword on this book, *Daily Manna (food for the hungry soul).* In this day and age much emphasis is placed on food and the satisfaction of the physical appetite, forgetting the most important need of man which is food for the soul.

Being in Pastoral Ministry for over twenty years, I've read books written on several other subjects, which have served well as information. Dr. Ronnie Whittier with earned Doctorate degrees in Theology and Religious Education has written this book not just for reading; but it's considered a Handbook for daily living, which includes principles for enforcing and strengthening our Christian walk. Sound doctrine matters if we are to stay on course and fulfill the purpose God has called us unto.

Dr. Whittier has placed within this book special emphasis on Believers being empowered through the Baptism of the Holy Ghost as seen demonstrated in his own life and ministry, causing tremendous church growth.

The foundation chapter, Christian Disciplines all based on the Word of God is a proper guideline helping our walk in proper regard for growing daily in God.

As you read on, it gets deeper and more informative as your appetite for *Daily Manna* gets stronger every day. As we are filled with food for our souls we would be prompted to have others spiritually fed so they too can experience that soul satisfying meal provided.

May God enrich every reader's soul bountifully as they too feast on *Daily Manna.*

- Pastor Phillip Parasram
Bethel Pentecostal Ministries
Guyana, South America

Series 1:

Am I Blessed or Not?

Lesson 1:

A Question Of Recognition

Scripture Text:
Jeremiah 29:11; Romans 8:28; 2 Corinthians 9:8

There dwelling within our inner man is the question, Am I blessed or not? What we sometimes classify as a setback in blessings could very well be a setup for blessings. The base reason for this question lies within our inability to recognize the handiwork of God. On our journey in life we experience situations that cause questions of doubt and skepticism. We become accustomed to negative or stagnant feedback. We accept bad advice from well-meaning people. We stop listening for the voice and leading of God and we try to make things happen our way and in our timing.

Recently, I asked a question to a class. I asked for the definition of the word blessing. I noticed a silence and also a look of uncertainty on the face of some people. This inspired me to dig deeper into this subject matter. My initial belief is that many are hindered by a question of recognition. They're not clear on what or why so they fail to recognize a move of God in their life. There are many underlying reasons that lead to unclear perception in seeing your outpouring of blessings:

I. Complacency is a major contributor to the abortion of blessings.

II. A lack of knowledge in regards to who you are in God.

III. A lack of faith.

IV. A weak prayer-life.

V. Misguided faith.

VI. A lack of patience.

VII. A non-repentant heart.

VIII. Negative surroundings of people.

IX. Lack of obedience to the leading of God.

X. Desire in your life for things that God opposes.

The steps of a good man are ordered by the LORD: and he delighteth in his way.

Though he fall, he shall not be utter cast down: for the LORD upholdeth him with his hand.

He is ever merciful, and lendeth: and his seed is blessed. **(Psalms 37:23-25)**

Summary:

Life is too short for us to spend quality time wrestling with questions that the Word of God has already answered. There is no question as to whether God loves us enough to give us endless and bountiful blessings. We must align ourselves with the promises of assurance ordained by God. Hopefully, we will arrive at a point in our walk with God that all questions of whether we are blessed or not has vanished. Our lives should be our testimony.

Lesson 2:

Exceeding Abundantly Blessed!

Scripture Text:
Ephesians 3:20; Psalms 1:1-3

Before engaging upon this subject, the fact that we are indeed blessed should have already been established. Within the confines of Christendom we have a tendency to categorize certain blessings on a particular level. With this thought in mind we can sometimes unknowingly downplay the everyday blessings bestowed upon us by our Heavenly Father. Before we can enter into the realm of exceeding abundantly, it is of grave importance to be grateful for the common and sometimes overlooked blessings we experience every day. I want to caution us to remember that God owes us nothing, but we owe Him everything. It is also important to remember that our love for God and our servitude to Him should not be based on material things we hope to receive.

Exceeding Abundantly Blessed is the result of not only good works, but pure and unadulterated love for God. There are obvious characteristics of an exceeding abundantly blessed person:

I. They display an unprecedented love for God.

II. They have a deep love for the people of God.

III. They have a never-ending desire to do Kingdom Building work.

IV. They make sacrifices of all kinds to make sure God comes first in all they do.

V. They study to know, love, and live God's Word daily.

VI. They share the gospel with others no matter what the cost.

VII. They are soul-winners for the Kingdom.

VIII. They hunger and thirst after righteousness.

IX. They are peace-makers.

X. They support the work of God financially, if at all possible.

XI. They are not selfish people.

XI. They are Visionaries

I would that you prosper and be in health even as your soul prospers.

(3 John 1:2)

Summary:

Being Exceeding Abundantly Blessed is not determined by how much you own. An individual that has an abundance of the love of God is an abundantly blessed person. All of the material things in life that comes along with such a godly lifestyle will not deter or break the focus of such a person.

Lesson 3:

Internalizing and Personalizing Your Blessings!

Scripture Text:
Psalms 103:1-5, 22; Romans 12:1-2

In a world consisting of roughly 6-7 billion people; it may be hard to believe that God is giving special attention to you. It can be challenging to your faith. You ask yourself questions like, "What's so special about me? Why does God care so much for me? Why does He love me so?"

We must learn to accept the sovereignty of the love of God. When Christ came into this world of sin, He told us that God so loved the world.**(St. John 3:16)** That includes you!

In God's sovereignty, He has the capability to personally love each and every one of us at the same time. Sometimes we mistakably restrict God to man's limitations. Within our study "Am I Blessed or Not", we must learn to **internalize and personalize** our blessings. This protects us from allowing present troubles to dominate our thought life. We know God loves us all, but there are times you must see His love as a personal touch, a special sign that you are His dearly beloved. There are many benefits to internalizing and personalizing blessings from God:

I. His presence will not be difficult to detect.

II. He will reveal even more blessings you never knew existed within your life.

III. You are less prone to complain about things going on in your life.

IV. You don't feel the void of being alone.

V. You testify more of the power of God.

VI. You are excited to share your personal story as a means of encouragement.

VII. You spend more personal time developing your relationship with Him.

VIII. Your Christian light shines brighter.

Summary:

All of us from time to time must be reminded that our Heavenly Father is yet at work in our lives. We become so driven by our carnal endeavors that we miss the spiritual edification awarded to us by our experiences.

God allows certain things to unfold in our lives that He may reveal His purpose for us. The mistake of giving too much attention to the blessings of others causes one to unwittingly belittle the blessing afforded to self.

This is not a summons to become selfish. It is a call for us to acknowledge the move of God in our own lives. Whether you are willing to admit it or not, you are indeed happy to see others blessed. But, you must also internalize and personalize blessings going on in your walk with God.

Lesson 4:

The Blessing of Being a Blessing!

Scripture Text:
Luke 6:35-38, I Cor. 13:4-5, Ephesians 4:32

The initial purpose of this series was for us to arrive at a point in our everyday life where we can recognize our daily blessings. If an individual is still struggling with the question of whether they are blessed or not, they will find it even more difficult to see where they can be a blessing to others. The first goal for many believers is to get pass the "poor old me" syndrome. When harboring such negative thoughts, one has the tendency to close self out from the ability to be used by God, even to be blessing or an answered prayer to someone else. God is not restricted or limited to only blessing you; He desires to make you a channel through which He can bless others. There are many ways your blessed life can bless other people:

I. You must realize you are consistently blessed to be a blessing.

II. Purpose every day to make someone else day a brighter day.

III. Be an Intercessory Prayer Warrior.

IV. Share your story with others.

V. Be an Encourager.

VI. Be a Giver.

VII. Fellowship with others so they may adopt your positive ways.

VIII. Share the Word of God with them.

IX. Listen to them attentively, then have them attentively listen.

X. Always initiate positive perspective to any and all matters.

Summary:

It can sometimes be quite difficult for you to see how you can bless others. When you find yourself searching for answers to your issues in life, try being to others what you hope others could be to you. Pray that God will make you the lender and not the borrower. Give and it shall be given to you.

(St. Luke 6:38)

Lesson 5:

Unseen Daily Blessings!

Scripture Text:
St. Matt. 6:11; St. Luke 11:3; Colossians 1:16; Hebrews 11:3

We get into a mode of believing that a blessing is something we can readily see. If we can't see it happening or if there is no immediate evidence that it has happened, we drift back into complacency.

The assumption that we will see everything God is doing in our lives causes a dampening of faith. We assume that we are experiencing a drought in regards to blessings. According to scripture, there is an invisible world that many of us are not knowledgeable of **(Romans 1:20)**.

It is long overdue for Christians to rise to a level of spirituality wherein they can sense the handiwork of God even in the invisible world. This acquired level of spiritual insight heightens our awareness of a move of God.

Unseen daily blessings are not always easily identified; however, that does not negate the legitimacy of their existence. Take time to examine all those unmentioned blessings that occur in your life daily. Those unmentioned blessings are worth looking into. They are the fillers to all the other wonderful things God is doing in your life. Know this:

I. God is ordering your steps. (**Psalms 37:23**)

II. God gives overcoming testimonies that thwart heaviness. (**Rev. 12:11**)

III. The seed of God's Word continuously produce an inner growth. (**Jer. 20:9**)

IV. You're in the hands of God and no one can pluck you out. (**John. 10:28-29**)

V. You are part of a royal family. (**I Peter 2:9**)

VI. Your life is a light. (**St. Matt.5:14**)

VII. The devil can only trouble you to a certain extent as God allow. (**Job 1:10**)

VIII. You have power over the power of the enemy. (**St. Luke 10:19**)

IX. Whatever the present trial, God has promised you good. (**Psalms 23:6**)

X. God is your very present help. (**Psalms 46:1**)

Summary:

It is within the nature of man to overlook the less obvious. You are not any less blessed if you cannot see what God is doing in your spiritual world. When you do arrive at that place in God where you can recognize the hand of God in your spiritual world, you are less prone to assume your blessings are few. Unseen blessings are not any less of a blessing than is natural blessings however, unseen blessings are sometimes harder to detect. We must learn to walk by faith and not by sight. **(II Cor. 5:7)**

Lesson 6:

Corporate Blessings!

Scripture Text:
Acts 2:39-47

God is such a loving and merciful God. He smiles not only on a few of us, but on all of us. There are times when we experience individualized blessings and then there are times when we experience **corporate blessings**. Individualized blessings are those blessings that God designs to encourage and strengthen you as an individual (personally). **Corporate blessings** are those blessings designed by God to encourage and strengthen a group of people (generally).

The blessings of the Lord are so phenomenal that it's difficult for some Christians to restrict personal blessings to self. As a result of sharing their testimony with other believers, the personal blessing becomes an encouragement and blessing to all. For the sake of identifying one from the other, we will focus on **corporate blessings** in this lesson. God showers blessings on the general body of believers for multiple reasons and purposes; we will seek to identify only a few.

Corporate blessings:

I. Help develop cohesion and unity within the body of believers.

II. Reveal the love of God from God for all body of Christians.

III. Reveal the necessity of love exemplified from one Christian to another.

IV. Promote a desire for unity within each member's household.

V. Encourage Intercessory Prayer within the church body.

VI. Enhances Corporate Prayer within the church body.

VII. Encourage Corporate Fasting within the church body.

VIII. Protect the integrity of the church body.

IX. Dismisses doubt, fear and unbelief.

X. Gives clarity to the vision of the ministry.

XI. Establishes purpose.

XII. Rewards the faithful.

XIII. Draws the skeptic and unbeliever to Christ.

Summary:

In the Holy Scriptures we discover **Corporate Blessings** of God heavily upon groups of people that comply to His Word. We see enemy put to flight, diseases cured, famines ended, walls torn down and walls built up. We see wars won and kingdoms reestablished. God is yet moving and a very present help in our time. Nothing would our God hold from us if we walk uprightly before Him.

Lesson 7:

Blessed Beyond The Grave!

Scripture Text:
Philippians 1:21; Proverbs 22:1; Ecclesiastes 7:1

We live our lives every day in anticipation that each day will bring with it the blessing above all blessings. Our greatest hope as Christians is that God will soon rapture His Church from this world of rapid decline. In the meantime, we try to live our lives in such a manner that it pleases God the Father. We learn to cope with societal problems and pray our way through difficult times.

A truly regenerated and born-again Christian understands the ramifications of professing their salvation and hope of a better place than this world. They may experience being laughed at and told they are only living a pipe dream.

The truth of the matter for the Christian is that they are blessed in this life to have a relationship with our Lord and Savior Jesus Christ. They are also blessed in the world to come by a reward of eternal life with God the Father.

On the matter of material blessings, not only are they blessed while they are here in this life. They have the security of knowing, if their children will practice the godly principles passed on by the parents, they will inherit blessings as well. The true Christian is blessed beyond the grave in a number of ways:

I. They leave a legacy of godly living because of how they lived.

II. God promised to bless their seed if their seed holds to godliness.

III. Their treasures were stored in heaven and not on earth.

IV. They will no longer be subject to the sorrows of this world.

V. They will live with Christ in a sin free society called heaven.

VI. They leave believing loved ones with a hope of seeing them again.

VII. Death is not the end; it's a new beginning for them.

VIII. Their name is synonymous with godliness.

IX. When God calls them home it indicates they finished their task.

Summary:

Finding peace and solitude in anticipating blessings beyond the grave may seem ludicrous to an unbeliever. But to know Christ and to have lived each day of your living years to His glory is a legacy the believer longs to leave behind. We come to know and understand that life on earth is but for a short while. All those material things we work so hard to own in this life becomes secondary and of little interest. Where we are headed promises far greater satisfaction than the temporary pleasures we have in this life. There are blessings that reach far beyond the grave and our only chance of enjoying those blessings lie in our love and loyalty to our Lord and Savior Jesus Christ.

Lesson 8:

Yes, I am Blessed!

Scripture Text: **Various Scriptures**

We have become accustomed to a very busy and sometimes overwhelming society. We have subconsciously taught ourselves to jump aboard the vehicle of life and hope it lands us in a better place. The question throughout our lives has been an inner struggle not always shared with others, the question of "Am I blessed or not?"

Many want to believe they are doing just fine in their Christian profession. Deep down inside they are wrestling with not only how they see themselves, but how they are seen by others as well. We have made a detailed effort in our series of "Am I blessed?" to point out the many facts that prove we are indeed blessed in more ways than we can possibly know.

We began our series with stating the obvious:

I. It's a question of recognition in regards to how blessed you are. **(II Cor. 9:8)**

II. You are Exceedingly Abundantly Blessed. **(Ephesians 3:20)**

III. You must internalize and personalize your blessings. **(Psalms 103:1-5)**

IV. You must realize there are unseen daily blessings. **(Colossians 1:16)**

V. You are blessed to be a blessing. **(St. Matt. 9:35-38)**

VI. You are part of a corporate blessing. **(Acts 2:39-47)**

VII. You are blessed beyond the grave. **(Ecclesiastes 7:1)**

Summary:

We have engaged ourselves in a series of truths hopefully solidifying the reality of our unmerited blessings. No doubt your present state of mind still questions the validity of how blessed a person you are.

You are probably still in debt to creditors, aching with pain in your body, troubled on your job or looking for a job. You might yet be in the middle of domestic complications and you might be asking yourself what is the purpose of your being?

My answer to you is for you to stop and think about the many people in life that were not able to cope with what life dealt to them and gave up on it all. You are still hopeful even in the midst of it all. Not because of your own abilities; but because of the long reaching arm of God and the longsuffering love of God extended to you.

Yes, it’s another of the blessings of God sometimes unnoticed due to the high expectations of our flesh and the ungrateful need to feel approved by others. God has smiled on all of us whether we acknowledge it or not. He has poured from the cup of mercy and grace bountiful blessings. It would benefit us all to slow down and give praise to our Heavenly Father. We are blessed without measure in many ways. So when you ask yourself the question, am I blessed? Think of God’s goodness and all He’s done for you. Then you should readily say I am blessed, I’m blessed indeed!

Series 2:

Who is the Holy Ghost?

Lesson 1:

Who is the Holy Ghost?

The Bible calls the Holy Ghost the Spirit of the Father **(Matt. 10:20)**; and the Spirit of God. **(I Cor. 3:16; Acts 2:17)** The Holy Ghost is that part of God that is specifically related to human kind. In almost every instance in the Bible, the Holy Ghost is God in relation to human beings.

I. The Holy Ghost is a Person.

   A. He has intelligence. **(I Cor. 2:10-11; Rom 8:27; I Cor. 2:13)**

   B. He shows feelings. **(Eph. 4:30)**

   C. He has a will. **(I Cor. 12:11; Acts 16:6-11)**

II. He is God.

   A. He is related by name to the other two Persons of the Trinity. **(Acts 16:7; I Cor. 6:11; John 14:16)**

   B. His attributes are those that belong to God alone. **(Isaiah 40:13; I Cor. 2:12; Ps. 139:7; Job 33:4; Ps. 104:30)**

   C. His actions are those that only God alone can perform. **(Luke 1:35; 2 Peter 1:21; Gen.1:2)**

III. He is the fulfillment of Old and New Testament prophecy. **(Joel 2:28-29; St. Matt. 1:18-23; 3:11; Acts 1: 1-8; 2:14-21)**

Summary:

Genuine personality possesses intelligence, feelings, and will, and since the Holy Ghost has these attributes we can conclude that He is a Person. The Person of the Holy Ghost is very much alive as He is intricately interwoven in the Person of Christ.

Lesson 2:

The Work of the Holy Ghost!!!

The Work of the Holy Ghost is an important factor in the accomplishment of salvation, Christian experience, ministering to the world, understanding scriptures and to knowing Christ.

I. The Holy Ghost reveals the need for salvation.

   A. Peter and the apostles proclaimed this truth. **(Acts 5:29-32)**

   B. Jesus, the Son proclaimed this truth. **(John 16:8)**

   C. God, the Father, proclaimed this truth. **(Gen. 6:3)**

II. The Holy Ghost minister to the spiritual needs of the believer.

   A. He regenerates the believer. **(John 3:3-8; 6:63; Titus 3:5)**

   B. He indwells the believer. **(John 14:17; Romans 8:9; I Cor. 3:16; 6:19)**

   C. He baptizes the believer. **(Acts 1:5; 11:16; I Cor.12:13)**

   D. He seals the believer. **(Eph.1:13; 4:30; II Cor. 1:22; Gal.4:6)**

III. The Holy Ghost is the author of scripture.

   A. Men spoke as they were moved by the Holy Ghost **(2 Pet. 1:21)**.

B. The Holy Ghost speak to churches. **(Rev. 2:7, 11)**

IV. Jesus was conceived of the Holy Ghost. **(Luke 1:35)**

A. The Holy Ghost anointed Jesus at baptism. **(Matt. 3:16)**

B. The Holy Ghost was active in Jesus' death and resurrection. **(Heb. 9:14; Rom. 1:4; 8:11)**

Summary:

The Holy Ghost does a blessed work in the life of each believer and the work of His ministry should not be restrained due to the presence of sin. The Spirit of God will make Himself known as long as the believer's life is godly aligned.

Lesson 3:

The Gift of the Holy Ghost

Then Peter said unto them, repent, be baptized every one of you in the name of Jesus Christ for the remission of your sins, and you shall receive **the gift of the Holy Ghost**. For the **promise** is unto you, to your children, to all that are afar off, even as many as the Lord our God shall call. **(Acts 2:38-39)**

I. The Holy Ghost is a **gift** from God **promised** to **every** believer. (**Acts 18:4-16; Acts 19:1-7; Eph. 1:13; Acts 10:44-48; John 7:38-39; Mark 1:8; Acts 2:14-17**)

II. There is **one** Holy Ghost, but there are nine *(foundational)* gifts (*meaning there are many other gifts springing from those gifts mentioned by the apostle Paul)* (**I Cor. 12:4-11**), and nine fruit exemplified of the Holy Spirit. (**Gal. 5:22-23**)

III. The Holy Ghost is a gift not a reward. (**Eph. 2:8-9; Gal. 4:6; John 15:26**)

IV. God promised to pour out His Spirit in the last days. **(Joel 2:28-29; Acts 2:16-18)**

V. God is not slack concerning His promise. **(2 Peter 3:9; Romans 4:20-21**)

Summary:

Don't allow worldly skepticism to convince you to believe that God no longer fill people with the gift of the Holy Ghost. For whatsoever things were written aforetime were written for our learning, that we through patience and comfort of the scriptures might have hope. (**Romans 15:4**)

Lesson 4:

Evident Signs of the Indwelling Holy Ghost!!!

When an individual has the indwelling of the Holy Ghost there are evident signs of a divine order. The indwelling produces a new life of love, actions, ambitions and earnest expectations. The old man has passed away and all things have become new.

I. The indwelling produces love. **(I John 4:19)**

II. The indwelling produces actions. **(Gal. 5:16 -18)**

III. The indwelling produces ambitions. **(John 6:27)**

IV. The indwelling produces earnest expectations. **(Philippians 1:20-21)**

V. The indwelling reveals a truly born-again believer. **(St. John 13:34-35; II Cor. 5:17; I Cor. 6:20)**

Summary:

There are evident signs of the indwelling Holy Ghost made manifest in the lives of individuals that are truly committed to their walk with the Lord.

Lesson 5:

Every Believer Should Be Holy Ghost Filled!!!

Believers who are filled with the Holy Ghost have an unnatural capacity to be disciplined in spiritual organization. They have a supernatural ability that only Lord God of Heaven can ordain in a believers life. Many religious denominations make the grave mistake of teaching that not all believers need to be Holy Ghost filled.

If a believer is going to be effective in his or her walk with the Lord they must accept the scriptural teaching of being filled with the Holy Ghost. **(John 7:38-39)** We were not born with the Holy Ghost already in us because scripture teaches we were born with a sinful nature **(Psalms 58:3; Psalms 51:5; St. John 3:3-7).**

I. The Holy Ghost initiates change and power in the life of a believer. This change is not a self-induced change. **(Acts 1:5, 8)**

II. Not all believers are full of the Holy Ghost. (Being filled with the Holy Ghost is not the same as being full of the Holy Ghost). **(Acts 6:3-8; 7:55; Gal. 3:1-3)**

II. A believer must spend quality time in prayer to develop sensitivity to the leading of the Holy Ghost. **(Jas. 5:16)**

III. A sincere believer does not reject the knowledge of the Holy Ghost. (**Hosea 4:6; b: Acts 19:1-6**)

IV. The skeptical believer makes non-scriptural excuses; not accepting the teaching of being Holy Ghost filled. **(Rom. 1:16-20)**

Summary:

By believing and not doubting the canonicity of scripture, many have received the precious gift of the Holy Ghost. Rather than arguing with scripture, ask God for understanding and obedience to this much neglected and disregarded truth. Seek and you shall find. **(Matt. 6:33)**

Lesson 6:

Being Holy Ghost Filled Produces Lasting Results!!!

(Conclusion of Series)

Unlike man-made materials that supposedly guarantee certain results for a life-time; the Holy Ghost is sure to fulfill His claim. There is much joy talk about the effects one is to experience when filled with the Holy Ghost. The talk seems to dwindle into the distant past after a flurry of trials are encountered. The Believer must come to understand that being Holy Ghost filled is not a short-term fix to life's issues. We must be mindful that the Holy Ghost is in essence a keeping power that will never leave nor forsake you. Jesus promised that after receiving the Holy Ghost, you will be guided into all truth **(St. John 14:26; 16:13,33).** He produces lasting results in the believer's life **(St. Matt. 28:20)**.

I. He has a will and we must always obey and submit to it. **(I Samuel 15:22)**

II. His actions are those that only God alone can perform. **(Philippians 1:6)**

IV. A believer must spend quality time in prayer to develop sensitivity to the leading of the Holy Ghost. **(James 5:16)**

V. The indwelling Holy Ghost produces earnest expectations. **(Philippians 1:20-21)**

VI. Don't become unraveled because your life is under attack by Satan. **(II Cor. 4:8-11)**

VII. The Holy Ghost will empower you to be victorious in all things. **(Philippians 4:13)**

VIII. The Holy Ghost generates within the believer uncommon resilience. **(Romans 8:31-39)**

Summary:

When an individual has the indwelling of the Holy Ghost there are evident signs of a divine order. The indwelling produces a new life of love, actions, ambitions and earnest expectations. The old man has passed away and all things have become new.

(II Cor. 5:17)

Series 3:

The Spiritual Disciplines

Lesson 1:

The Spiritual Disciplines

The doctrine of instant satisfaction is a primary spiritual problem. The desperate need today is not for a greater number of intelligent people, or gifted people, but for a deep people. Spiritual Discipline exercised in the midst of our relationships with our husband or wife, our brothers and sisters, our friends and neighbors produces depth.

I. The primary requirement is a longing for God. **(Ps. 42:1-2; St. Matt. 6:33)**

II. Spiritual growth is the purpose of the Disciplines. **(II Peter 3:18; I Peter 3:18; Eph. 4:15)**

III. Spiritual Disciplines establishes good character. **(I Cor. 9:27; Romans 8:12-13; Col. 3:5-10)**

IV. Spiritual Disciplines are exercises in righteousness. **(II Cor. 3:6; Romans 5:17)**

Summary:

The classical disciplines of the spiritual life call us to move beyond surface living into the depths.

Lesson 2:

The Discipline of Meditation

In contemporary society our Adversary majors in three things; noise, hurry, and crowds. If he can keep us engaged in "muchness" and "manyness" he will rest satisfied. If we hope to move beyond the superficialities of our culture, including our religious culture, we must be willing to exercise the discipline of meditation. The discipline of meditation was certainly familiar to the authors of Scripture. (**Gen. 24:63; Ps. 63:6; Ps. 119:148; Ps. 1:2**)

I. Christian meditation is the ability to hear God's voice and obey. (**Exod. 33:11; Exod. 20:19; John 5:19,30**)

II. Repentance and obedience are essentials of meditation. (**Ps. 119:97, 101, 102**)

III. Meditation of Scripture will internalize and personalize. (**Rev. 3:20; Jn. 14:14-15, 27**)

IV. Meditate on the handiwork of the Lord our God. (**Ps. 19:1; Job 38-41**)

Summary:

The Discipline of Meditation will arouse spiritual depth in the life of the sincere Christian. If you are going to grow as a Christian you must internalize and personalize God's Word. What happens on the inside will soon materialize itself on the outside.

Quiz for Lessons 1-2

The Spiritual Disciplines

Scripture Text:
(II Timothy 2:15)

1. Name at least five spiritual disciplines.

2. How does one produce depth in spiritual disciplines?

3. What 3 things does the enemy use to hinder our growth?

4. The desperate need today is for a ________ people.

5. _________ of Scripture will ________ and personalize.

6. The doctrine of ________ satisfaction is a primary spiritual problem.

7. Repentance and _________ are essentials of meditation.

8. Spiritual Disciplines are exercises in ___________

9. What is the purpose of the Disciplines? Give Scripture reference.

10. Spiritual Disciplines establish ________ character.

11. What is the primary requirement for spiritual discipline?

12. What is the ability to hear God's voice and obey?

____

____

____

____

____

____

____

Lesson 3:

The Discipline of Prayer

In prayer, real prayer, we begin to think God thoughts after Him: to desire the things He desires, to love the things He loves, to will the things He wills. God slowly and graciously reveals to us our evasive actions and sets us free from them. Prayer is the central avenue God uses to transform us.

I. Real prayer is something we learn. (**St. Matt. 6:5-13; Luke 11:1-9**)

II. Prayer is an important ingredient for godly intimacy. (**Mark 1:35; Ps. 63:1: Acts 6:4**)

III. We must allow the Holy Spirit to pray through us. (**Rom. 8:26- 28**)

IV. We must pray a covering blessing upon our children. (**Mark 10:13-16**)

V. We should pray for those in authority. (**I Tim. 2:1-4**)

VI. We must pray one for another. (**Jas. 5:16; Acts 2:1**)

VII We must pray without ceasing. (**Eph. 6:18; I Thess. 5:17**)

VIII. Prayer works (**Is. 38:1-8; Jas. 5:16-18**)

Summary:

The strongest motive in prayer is the glorification of God and the vindication of His power and character.

Lesson 4:

The Discipline of Fasting

Throughout Scripture fasting refers to abstaining from food for spiritual purposes. It stands in distinction to the hunger strike and health dieting which stresses abstinence from food for physical and political, not spiritual purposes. In most cases fasting is a private matter between the individual and God.

I. Fasting is found throughout the Scriptures. (**Lev. 23:7; Joel 2:15; II Chron. 20:1-4; Zech. 8:19; Luke 18:12; II Cor. 11:27**)

II. Fasting is a necessary discipline. (**Matt. 6:16; Matt. 9:15; Acts 13:2-3; Ezra 8:21**)

III. Fast with the right motives while centering on God. (**Matt. 6:16-18; Luke 2:37; Acts 13:2; Zech. 7:5; I Cor. 6:12; I Cor. 9:27; Ps. 35:13**)

IV. Fasting can bring breakthrough in the spiritual realm. (**St. Matt. 17:14-21; Ps. 69:10; Matt. 4:1-11**)

V. Fasting manifests earnestness to God. **(I Cor. 7:5)**

Summary:

Faith needs prayer for its development and full growth, and prayer needs fasting for the same reasons.

Lesson 5:

The Discipline of Study

The purpose of the Spiritual Disciplines is the total transformation of the person. They aim at replacing old destructive habits of thought with new life-giving habits. Nowhere is this purpose more clearly seen than in the Discipline of Study. Study is a specific kind of experience in which through careful attention to reality the mind is enabled to move in a certain direction. The Discipline of study involves five necessary steps:

I. The Discipline of Study involves repetition. (**Deut. 11:18; Ps. 119:104; Prov. 14:8**)

II. The Discipline of Study involves concentration. (**Prov. 15:28; Phil. 4:8**)

III. The Discipline of Study involves comprehension. (**Prov. 4:7; Prov. 12:1; John 8:32**)

IV. The Discipline of Study involves reflection. (**Prov. 14:6; Romans 12:2; St. John 17:3**)

V. The Discipline of Study involves God. (**Matt. 7:7-8; II Tim. 2:15**)

Summary:

Most people assume that because they know how to read words they know how to study. Application of repetition, concentration, comprehension, reflection and a sincere desire to know God are all essentials in the Discipline of Study. These five points are applicable to Christian Discipline, yet they transcend secular barriers as well.

Quiz for Lessons 3-5

The Spiritual Disciplines

Scripture Text:
(II Timothy 2:15)

1. Prayer is an important ___________ for godly _________.

2. What is the central avenue God uses to transform us?

3. What does prayer need for development and growth?

4. Give a scripture reference to praying for our children.

5. Fasting is a __________ discipline.

6. Name three essentials of the discipline of study.

7. What is the strongest motive in prayer?

8._______ is a private matter between an individual and God.

9. Which of the disciplines help the mind seek direction?

10. According to **I Tim.2:1-4** we should _______________.

11. According to **I Cor.7:5** fasting __________________.

12. What two disciplines that are the focus of **St. Matt.17:21**?

13. What are the 5 necessary steps in the Discipline of Study?

____

____

____

____

____

____

____

Lesson 6:

The Discipline of Simplicity

The preacher of Ecclesiastes observes that "God made man simple; man's complex problems are of his own devising". (**Eccles.7:29**) Constantly the Bible deals decisively with the inner spirit of slavery that an idolatrous attachment to wealth brings. "If riches increase, set not your heart on them, "says the psalmist. (**Ps.62:10**) No servant can serve two masters, for either he will hate the one and love the other, or he will be devoted to the one and despise the other. You cannot serve God and mammon (Aramaic for wealth). (**Luke 16:13**)

I. Simplicity knows contentment in both abasement and abounding. (**Phil. 4:12; Matt. 5:37**)

II. Your life does not consist in the abundance of your possessions. (**Luke 12:15; Luke 12:33; Matt. 13:45-46; Matt. 19:16-22**)

III. The Discipline of Simplicity provides proper perspective. (**Deut. 8:7-9; Deut. 8:17; Ps. 24:1**)

IV. He who trusts in his riches shall fall. (**Prov. 11:28; Mk. 10:17-27**)

V. The Discipline of Simplicity is to first seek the kingdom of God. (**Matt. 6:25-33**)

Summary:

May God give us the courage, the wisdom, the strength always to hold the kingdom of God as the number-one priority of our lives. To do so is to live in simplicity.

Lesson 7:

The Discipline of Solitude

Solitude is more a state of mind and heart than it is a place. There is solitude of the heart that can be maintained at all times. Crowds, or the lack of them, have little to do with this inward attentiveness. In the midst of noise and confusion we are settled into a deep inner silence. We always carry with us a portable sanctuary of the heart. The wise preacher of Ecclesiastes says that there is a "time to keep silence and a time to speak". (**Eccles. 3:7**)

I. Jesus frequently practiced outward solitude. (**Matt. 4:1-11; Matt. 14:23; Mk. 1:35; Luke 5:16**)

II. Jesus included the disciples in the practice of solitude. (**Mark 6:31; Matt. 17:1-9**)

III. Solitude and silence are compatible disciplines. (**James 3:1-12; Eccles. 5:1-2; Matt. 26:36-46**)

III. Use this time to reevaluate your objectives and goals in life. (**Luke 14:28; Prov. 6:6-11**)

V. The fruit of solitude is the increased sensitivity and compassion for others. (**Matt. 9:35-38; Matt. 5:6-7; Heb. 10:24-25**)

Summary:

Inward solitude has outward manifestations. There is the freedom to be alone, not in order to be away from people but in order to hear the divine Whisper better.

Lesson 8:

The Discipline of Submission

The obsession to demand that things go the way we want them to go is one of the greatest bondages in human society today. In the discipline of submission we are released to drop the matter, to forget it. Only in submission are we enabled to bring this spirit to a place where it no longer controls us. Only submission can free us sufficiently to enable us to distinguish between genuine issues and stubborn self-will.

I. The biblical view of Submission focuses on how we view others. (**I Peter 2:18, 21-23; Matt. 5:44; Matt. 10:39**)

II. Through Submission, leadership is found in becoming the servant of all. (**Phil. 2:18; Mark 9:35; Jn. 13:15**)

III. The Disciplines of Submission and Service function concurrently. (**James 1:27; Acts 9:16**)

IV. Submission is not a sign of weakness, but it's a sign of meekness. (**St. Matt. 5:5**)

V. The Discipline of Submission reminds us of both who we are and whose we are. (**I Cor. 6:19-20)**

Summary:

The most radical social teaching of Jesus was his total reversal of the contemporary notion of greatness. The average person is not willing to submit to the will of another. In our study we are simply emphasizing the desire one should have in submitting to the ultimate Will of God.

Quiz for Lessons 6-8

The Spiritual Disciplines

Scripture Text:
(II Timothy 2:15)

1. According to **Eccles. 7:29**, how did God make man and how are man's problems devised?

2. What is the Aramaic word for wealth according to one of our lessons?

3. There is a solitude of the ________ that can be maintained at all times.

4. According to **Eccles. 3:7**, there is a time to keep _________ and a time to __________.

5. What is one of the greatest bondages in human society today?

6. Give two scripture references to the biblical view of submission.

7. Contentment in both abasement and abounding is known through which spiritual discipline?

8. We always carry with us a portable _________ of the heart.

9. Which discipline reminds us of both who we are and whose we are? Give scripture reference.

10. Explain **Proverbs 11:28** in contrast to **Matt. 6:25-33**.

11. What was the most radical social teaching of Jesus?

12. The fruit of __________ is the increased sensitivity and compassion for others. Give one scripture reference.

Lesson 9:

The Discipline of Service

As the cross is the sign of submission, so the towel is the sign of service. When Jesus gathered his disciples for the Last Supper they were having trouble deciding who was the greatest. This was no new issue for them. **(Luke 9:46)**

Whenever there is trouble over who is the greatest, there is trouble over who is the least. Of all the classical Spiritual Disciplines, service is the most conducive to the growth of humility. When we set out on a consciously chosen course of action that accents the good of others and is for the most part, a hidden work, a deep change occurs in our spirits.

I. Jesus lived a life of servant-hood, thus exercising the Discipline of Service. (**St. John 13:14, 15; Matt. 20:25-28**)

II. Self-righteous Service is not True Service. (**Mark 9:35; I John 2:16; I Cor. 4:13; Gal. 6:2**)

III. There is a service of common courtesy. (**Titus 3:2; I Peter 4:9; I Tim.3:2; Titus 1:8**)

IV. There is the service of sharing the word of Life. (**James 2:8; Matt. 11:30; Rom. 1:15-17; Acts 2:42; Heb. 4:12**)

Summary:

Many people want to serve God, but only as advisers. Give yourself to God and giving to others will be easy and joyful. Be willing to pour water before looking to part water.

Lesson 10:

The Discipline of Confession

The Discipline of Confession helps the believer to grow into "mature manhood, to the measure of the stature of the fullness of Christ" (**Eph.4:13**). "But isn't confession a grace instead of a discipline ?" It is both. Unless God gives the Grace, no genuine confession can be made. But it is also a discipline because there are things we must do. It is a consciously chosen course of action that brings us under the shadow of the Almighty. Confession is a difficult discipline for us because we all too often view the believing community as a fellowship of saints before we see it as a fellowship of sinners. We hide ourselves from one another and live in veiled lies and hypocrisy.

I. We are to confess all of our sins to God. **(Lev. 5:4-6; Lev. 26:40-45; Prov. 28:13; I Jn.1:9)**

II. We are to confess our sins against one another to one another. **(Jas. 5:16; Gal. 6:1-3)**

III. We have God ordained authority to receive confessions and to forgive those who have sinned against us. **(John 20:23; Matt. 5:23-25; Matt. 6:12, 14-15)**

Summary:

An examination of conscience, true sorrow and a determination to avoid sin are all essentials of true confession. The Discipline of Confession can sometimes be challenging, but it is very rewarding when exercised in godly sincerity.

Quiz for Lessons 9-10

The Spiritual Disciplines

Scripture Text:
(II Timothy 2:15)

1. An examination of conscience, true__________ and a ______________ to avoid sin are all essentials of true ______________.

2. Why is confession a difficult discipline for us?

3. Many people want to serve God, but only as __________.

4. ____________ is both a __________ and a Discipline.

5. What hidden work causes a change in your spirit?

6. Explain Ephesians chapter four, verse number thirteen.

7. Explain Hebrews chapter number four verse number twelve.

8. What type of service is not true service?

9. Explain James chapter number five, verse number sixteen.

10. Which of the Disciplines is most conducive to humility?

Lesson 11:

The Discipline of Worship

To worship is to quicken the conscience by the holiness of God, to feed the mind with the truth of God, to purge the imagination by the beauty of God, to open the heart to the love of God, to devote the will to the purpose of God. It is to know, to feel, to experience the resurrected Christ in the midst of the gathered community. It is the human response to the divine initiative. Worship should be considered a Spiritual Discipline because it is an ordered way of acting and living that sets us before God so He can transform us.

I. God is actively seeking worshippers. (**St. John 4:23, 12:32**)

II. We are to worship God and no other. (**St. Matt. 4:10; Exod. 20:3**)

III. Worship must have priority in our lives. (**Mark 12:30; Ezek. 44:15**)

IV. Worship brings about a “holy expectancy”. (**Acts 2:2, 4:31, 5:1-11, 9:36-43, 20:7-10**)

V. There are proper avenues of preparation leading to worship. (**Rom. 8:4; Hab. 2:20; Heb. 13:15; I Pet. 2:5, 9; Acts 5:41; Acts 16:25; I Cor. 14:15; I Thess. 5:17; Matt. 5:23-24; Isa. 6:8; Col. 3:16**)

Summary:

Worship is a deliberate and disciplined adventure in reality. It involves an opening of ourselves to the adventurous life of the Spirit. It involves a willingness to let the word of Christ dwell in you richly.

Lesson 12:

The Discipline of Guidance

In our day heaven and earth are on tiptoe waiting for the emergence of a Spirit-led, Spirit-intoxicated, Spirit-empowered people. All of creation watches expectantly for the springing up of a spiritually disciplined people. Many are having a deep and profound experience of an Emmanuel of the Spirit-God with us; a knowledge that in the power of the Spirit, Jesus has come to **guide** his people himself. Not just individual guidance but corporate guidance as well.

I. The goal of guidance is conformity to the image of Christ. (**Romans 8:28b; 12:2 ;I Jn. 4:1**)

II. Guidance leads you into all truth. (**Prov. 3:5-6; Jn. 14:6;16:13;Acts 10:1-35**)

III. Spiritual Guidance is generated by obedience to Christ. (**Isaiah 1:17; 18-20**)

IV. Guidance of the Holy Spirit will open the right doors. (**Acts 16:6-10; II Cor. 2:12-17**)

Summary:

The Spirit that inspired the Scriptures will lead us in ways consistent with the Scriptures. God's ways is shaped and tempered by His self-revelation to us in the Bible.

Lesson 13:

The Discipline of Celebration
(Final Lesson in Spiritual Disciplines Series)

Celebration is a grace because it comes unmerited from the hand of God. It is also a discipline because there is work to be done. In Hebrews, we are instructed to "continually offer up a sacrifice of praise to God. That is the fruit of lips that acknowledge his name" (**Heb. 13:15**). The sacrifice of praise is the work to which we are called. Over a period of time you will discover what it really means to be 'God –intoxicated'.

I. Celebration Gives Strength to Life.
(**Leviticus 25:21; Nehemiah 8:10; Luke 2:10; John 15:11**)

II. Celebration is the path to joy.
(**Ps. 126:2; Matt. 6:25; Luke 11:27-28; Phil. 4:4-7**)

III. The Discipline of Celebration is a learned behavior.
(**Exodus 15:20; II Sam. 6:14,16**)

IV. Celebration honors the triumphant glory of God.
(**Exodus 15:1-2, 20-21**)

V. Celebration invokes outward expressions.
(**Luke 19:35-40; John 12:12-19; Acts 3:1-10; Revelation 19:1-8**)

Summary:

Celebration is the end result of the Spiritual Disciplines functioning in our lives. We will not know genuine celebration until there is a transforming work within us.

The Spiritual Disciplines

(Quiz for Lessons 1-13)

Scripture Text:
II Timothy 2:15

1. Name the 12 Spiritual Disciplines reviewed in our series.

2. What 3 things does the enemy use to hinder our growth?

3. What is the purpose of the Disciplines? Give Scripture reference.

4. Name three essentials of the discipline of study.

5. What is the strongest motive in prayer?

6. What are the 5 necessary steps in the Discipline of study?

7. What is the Aramaic word for wealth according to one of our lessons?

8. There is solitude of the _________ that can be maintained at all times.

9. According to Eccles.3:7, there is a time to keep _________ and a time to _________.

10. Which Discipline reminds us of both who we are and whose we are? Give scripture reference.

11. The fruit of __________ is the increased sensitivity and compassion for others. Give one scripture reference.

12. An examination of conscience, true__________ and a ______________ to avoid sin are all essentials of true ______________.

13. Why is confession a difficult discipline for us?

14. What does it mean to be "God–intoxicated"?

15. Explain Ephesians chapter four, verse number thirteen.

16. ___________ gives strength to life.

17. __________ is a deliberate and disciplined adventure in reality.

18. What Discipline is the human response to the divine initiative?

19. According to one of our lessons, how is God's ways shaped?

20. Name the 3 categories in which the 12 disciplines are divided.

    A.

    B.

    C.

Series 4:

The "I Am" Sayings of Christ

Lesson 1:

"I Am the Bread of Life"

Jesus said to them, "I AM the Bread of Life. He who comes to Me shall never hunger, and he who believes in Me shall never thirst…I am the living bread which came down from heaven. If anyone eats of this bread, he will live forever, and the bread that I shall give is My flesh, which I shall give for the life of the world." **(St. John 6:35, 51)**

Jesus affirmed three main things after designating Himself as life-giving bread:

I. His mission is one of doing the will of His Father. **(St. John 6:38)**

II. God has sent Him as the Bread of Life to give life to those to whom the Father has given the Son, not one of whom shall be lost. **(St. John 6:39)**

III. The purpose of God is that everyone who believes in the Son may have eternal life. **(St. John 6:40)**

Summary:

By recording the eight unique "I AM" sayings of Jesus, all of which are powerful expressions of His saving relationship to the world, the Beloved Disciple (John) brings us to a fuller understanding of the God-man as both protector and nurturer of His people.

Lesson 2:

"I Am the Light of the World"

"Light" is a metaphor (a figure of speech denoting a likeness) for the truth of the Gospel/coming to salvation. St. John draws out the metaphor in **St. John 1:1-18**, where darkness is seen as being unable to overcome the light. Here we see that what is common to light communicates a deep truth that no amount of darkness can subdue the glory of God in Jesus Christ.

I. God's first Creation recorded in Scripture was light. **(Genesis 1:2-5)**

II. In scripture, darkness refers to spiritual blindness/lack of salvation. **(Ps. 107:10; Isaiah 60:2; John 3:19, 12:35, 36; Eph. 5:8; I Peter 2:9, I John 1:6)**

III. The light of Christ draws the unregenerate. **(John 1:4-5; John 8:12; II Cor. 4:3-4)**

IV. The light of Christ illuminates the regenerated. **(Matt. 5:14-16; I Thess. 5:4-5; Rev. 21:23)**

Summary:

Then Jesus again spoke unto them, saying, "I am the light of the world; he who follows Me will not walk in the darkness, but will have the Light of life." **(St. John 8:12)**

Lesson 3:

"I Am the Door (Sheep Gate)"

Scripture text:
St. John 10:1-10; Acts 4:8-12; I Tim.2:1-5; I John 1:1-5

On an average day in Israel, sheep could be found grazing in pastures and drinking from streams. Once night fell, however, the sheep were brought into the sheepfold- a structure commonly made of stone with briars atop the wall that served as impediments to thieves. This left the gate as the only proper entryway, and so a guardian was placed there.

The life that Jesus gives is both eternal and increasingly abundant for His redeemed. If one desires it, he or she must pass through the door of the Lord Jesus Christ. All others will find only the wide path that leads to destruction. **(St. Matt. 7:13; St. John 10:9-10)**

I. Jesus asserts that He is the door of the sheepfold. **(St. John 10:7)**

II. Jesus is referring to Himself as the heavenly gate/door. **(Gen. 28:17; Ps. 78:23; Ps. 118:20; St. John 10:1-6)**

III. Jesus is the only door through which salvation comes. **(St. John 10:9; 14:1-6)**

Summary:

I am the door; by me if any man enter in, he shall be saved, and shall go in and out, and find pasture.

(St. John 10:9)

Lesson 4:

"I Am the Good Shepherd"

Scripture references:
Psalms 23; St. John 10:11-31; Romans 5:1-2

Our objective in this particular study is to understand Jesus' role as the Good Shepherd of our souls. Amid the same dialogue discussed in the previous lesson, Jesus reveals Himself as the long awaited Shepherd King calling His sheep into the fold. Jesus proves Himself to be the true Shepherd, for His sheep know His voice and follow, while refusing to follow strangers (**St. Jn.10:1-5**) We will carefully exegete from our reference scriptures how Christ is truly and rightfully the Good Shepherd.

I. The Good Shepherd is unlike a hireling**. (Isaiah 40:11; St. John. 10:11-18)**
(The hireling abandons the sheep at the first sign of danger)

II. The Good Shepherd will defend His own**. (Psalms 78:70-72; St. John 10:15-18)**
(The good shepherd displays sacrificial care for his sheep)

III. The Good Shepherd has both Jew and Gentile sheep. **(Ezekiel 37:24; Micah 2:12; St. John 10:16)**
(The other sheep-not of this fold are those from without Judaism)

IV. The sheep belong to the Good Shepherd; not anyone else. **(St. John 21:15-18; I Peter 5:1-2)**

Summary:

Jesus likens the relationship between the good shepherd and the sheep with His relationship to the Father.

Lesson 5:

"I Am the Resurrection and the Life"

Scripture references:
St. John 11:1-44

In the idiom of that day, to be closely associated with an idea was to virtually be that idea **(I John 4:7-8).** Jesus is so connected to the power over death, so inextricably tied to the power of eternal life and resurrection, that He is saying " not only do I have the power to raise others from the dead, not only do I have the power to raise Myself from the dead, but I am the resurrection itself! I literally embody it."

I. Jesus embodies the resurrection and the life. **(St. John 1:1-5; Revelation 1:17-18)**

II. Abundant life begins at regeneration in the heart of every born again believer. **(St. John 10:10; 11:25-26)**

III. Eternal life is obtained only through Jesus Christ. **(Romans 6:23)**

IV. Resurrection of good people differs from that of evil people. **(St. John 5:29)**

Summary:

The One who is the resurrection and the life has the key to unlock the grave and the power of death, so that believers have nothing to fear from it.

Lesson 6:

"I Am the Way, the Truth and the Life"

Scripture references:
St. John 13:31-14:31

This particular "I Am" statement has multiple attributes associated with it, some of which we have seen and explored earlier in this series. Jesus begins the conversation at **(John 14:1)** by seeking to put the disciples' hearts at ease, assuring them that despite His absence He will return so that they will be reunited. Jesus adds that they know where He is going, as well as how to get there.

I. Without the Way there is no going. (Only one way (Jesus), not many ways exist to God) **(St. John 10:7-9; St.Matt. 7:13-14; St. Luke 13:24; Acts 4:12)**

II. Without the Truth there is no knowing. (Jesus is the truth of God) **(St. John 1:14; 8:32; 10:34-39; 13:18; 17:12; St. Luke 24:25-27; Mark 12:24)**

III. Without the Life there is no living. (Jesus is the sustainer of life) **(Psalm 55:22; Isaiah 53:5-6; St. John 1:4; 3:15; 11:25)**

Summary:

This three-fold "I Am" statement anticipates St. Paul on Mars Hill: "For in Him we live and move and have our being" **(Acts 17:28)**

Lesson 7:

"I Am the True Vine"

Scripture Reference:
St. John 15:1-17

The degree of productivity as a Christian is directly proportional to the depth of one's relationship with Christ. If one is barely connected to the vine, then little fruit will be produced. Some within the church (universally speaking) profess faith though they actually are dead wood. These fruitless branches will be cut off by the Lord, so that the church (universal) will bear more fruit.

I. Jesus Christ is the "True Vine". **(St. John 15:1; St. Matt. 20:1)**

II. Our productivity (or lack thereof) is tied to how close we are to Christ. **(St. John 15:5; 16:24; 17:13)**

III. Branches not bearing fruit must be cut off and burned. **(St. John 15:6; Matt.3:10-12)**

IV. True believers obey the Lord's commands, submitting to His Word. **(St. John 15:7-10; Acts 13:43; Jude 21)**

IV. Jesus set the model by His perfect obedience to the Father. **(St. John 15:9-13; 3:35;17:23,24,26)**

Summary:

By loving Jesus and remaining responsive to His Word, the Christian maintains an essential union and produces the fruit that God desires.

Lesson 8:

"Before Abraham Was, I Am"

Scripture ref.:
St. John 1:1-18; 8:31-59

What was Jesus saying about Himself in (**John 8:58**) (Before Abraham, was I Am)? That He was really, really old? Or that He was the very God who passed between the animal halves in covenant with Abraham (a Theophany) (**Gen.15:17-18**). The hatred of several Jews present began to boil. They thought that being born Jews, physical descendants of Abraham, meant they were automatically in the kingdom of God, needing no liberation whatsoever. Jesus flatly contradicts them, stating that they cannot be sons of God the Father and seek to kill His Son. It is an impossibility. Being a true son means being completely obedient. They could not see the Messiah, the I Am that I Am, because they did not abide in the Father.

I. Jesus existed before Abraham. **(Exod. 3:14-15; Micah 5:1-2; John 1:1)**

II. Jesus' "I Am" claim made Him equal to God (Jehovah- the Self-Existent One). **(Deut. 32:39; Isaiah 41:4; Isaiah 43:10)**

III. Some Jews viewed Jesus' "I Am" claim as blasphemy. **(John 8:59; Lev. 24:16)**

Summary:

The Jews reaction to "Before Abraham was, I Am," showed that they fully understand that Jesus was claiming equality with God the Father.

Series 5:

Knowing the Traps, Strategies, and Tactics of Satan

Lesson 1:

No Longer a Victim of Satanic Trickery!

Christians face a very manipulative and deceiving enemy. The enemy we face is not afraid to launch an attack on unsuspecting people of God. It is within the strategy of Satan to make the Christian feel hopeless and unable to break loose of his grip. With that line of thinking the Christian unwittingly becomes a victim of Satan as opposed to a fearless conqueror. The initial problem facing the Christian is becoming bound by an enemy that Christ has already defeated on Calvary's Cross over two-thousand years ago **(Eph. 4:8)**. When anyone is victim to something or someone this is an indication that they were at some point overtaken. God has given us power over the power of the enemy, so we are no longer subject to his victimizing tactics **(Mk. 6:7)**.

I. He whom the Son has made free is free indeed. **(St. John 8:36)**

II. The Christian weaponry outweighs that of Satan. **(II Cor. 10:4)**

III. Know the wicked devices (traps) of the enemy. **(II Cor. 2:11)**

IV. Exercise the spirit of discernment. **(Hebrews 5:14)**

V. Have a consistent prayer life. **(St. Luke 18:1; I Thess. 5:17)**

VI. Stay alert to the environment around you. **(St. Luke 11:44)**

VII. Be confident that you are victorious in God. **(Psalms 27:3)**

VIII. Stay busy doing Kingdom Building work (Example: witnessing to the unsaved and unbelievers). **(I Cor. 15:58)**

Summary:

A repetition of attacks by Satan should at some point alert the Christian to the enemy's approach. There should be an awareness and discernment that the enemy is devising a trap to victimize and drain you of your spirituality. When putting into action the eight pointers mentioned above, any serious minded Christian should walk away victoriously.

Lesson 2:

Satanic Strategies of Deception!

The word strategy is defined as a careful plan or method used to obtain a particular goal. In this lesson we will observe several strategies Satan sometimes uses in exerting deception against the people of God. This is not an exhaustive list of strategies the enemy uses, only the most frequent and evident ones. It is my prayer that no Christian will fall prey to any of them. We must be watchful and prayerful at all times. **(St. Matt. 26:41)** We must never forget that we are engaged in spiritual warfare and the enemy is taking no prisoners. He (Satan) knows his end is drawing nearer and nearer every second, so his mission is to steal, kill and destroy. **(St. John 10:10)** Knowledge of satanic deception is most advantageous. **(II Cor. 2:11)**

I. Satan will fill your head with lies if you listen. **(Gen. 2:17; 3:4)**

II. Satan will fill your heart with anger. **(Gen. 4:8)**

III. Satan will fill your thoughts with envy. **(St. Matt. 27:18; Acts 7:9)**

IV. Satan will deceive your human emotions. **(Jeremiah 17:9)**

V. Satan will send a false love to win you over. **(Rev. 2:4)**

VI. He will tempt you to divert from God's Will. **(St. Matt. 4:3-4)**

VII. He will sow seed of discord amongst believers. **(Acts 15:1-3)**

VIII. He will use an overwhelming flurry of attacks. **(Acts 8:1b)**

IX. He will use a draining subtle attack against you. **(St. Luke 22:31)**

X. He will lead you to believe you're a lone warrior. **(I Kings 19:14-18)**

Summary:

We are required by God to be wise as serpents and harmless as doves. **(St. Matt. 10:16)** This is indicative of the truth that Satan is very skilled at what he does, seeing he took on the form of a serpent to deceive Eve in the Garden of Eden. The Devil is a master of deception and he has no problem exercising that skill on the saints of God. Deception is one of Satan's most used strategies to hinder a person's walk with God.

Lesson 3:

Satan's Scare Tactics!

Scripture Text:
Ephesians 6:10-13

As we engage upon this series, we will at times be confronted with passing thoughts that maybe we should avoid such a study. The truth behind this thought is that Satan is again using one of his scare tactics to thwart the idea of your becoming knowledgeable of his devices. **(II Cor. 2:11)**

Yes, we should be prayerful as we indulge in this study, but not with a sense of fear of what the enemy may do as a result of our learning to dismantle his tactics. God has not given us the spirit of fear, **(II Tim. 1:7)** so why should we allow Satan to frighten us? We must learn to discern very early the tactics of our adversary; otherwise he will position himself close enough to you to do a greater amount of damage.

Definition*:* Scare – to cause (someone) to become afraid; to frighten especially suddenly.

I. Satan will use an aggressive attack to strike you with fear.

II. Satan will use a loved one's threat of leaving you.

III. Satan will use sickness.

IV. Satan will use financial restraints against you.

V. Satan will use those in authority to oppress you.

VI. He will use family members (i.e. husband, wife, or children).

VII. He will promote self-degradation.

VIII. He will attack your mental stability.

IX. He will attack you in your dreams.

X. He will use the spirit of loneliness against you.

XI. He will threaten your character or integrity.

XII. Satan will even lead you to believe God is not pleased with you.

Summary:

No one enjoys being afraid. When a person is threatened by fear they take certain measures to overcome that fear. A scare tactic of Satan is to make you believe he has the power and ability to bypass the covering God has on your life. He uses scare tactics to challenge and disarm you of your faith in the sovereignty of our Almighty Protector and God.

Lesson 4:

Don't Give Opportunity (Place) to Satan!

Scripture Text:
Ephesians 4:27-32; 5:1

Definition: Opportunity -1. an amount of time or a situation in which something can be done. 2. a chance for advancement or progress.

If you listen to the voice of Satan he will entertain your thought-life with doubtful questions regarding godliness. Does it really take all this? Will one act of wrong- doing hurt anything? Am I depriving myself or being truthful with myself?

When you begin to answer those questions with statements such as; I deserve more and I'm going to make it happen my way! Satan has managed to get a foothold into your mind. You have given opportunity (place) to the devil.

Not only does Satan seek access by doubtful questions; he also uses everyday occurrences to infiltrate your walk with the Lord. The alert Christian is careful to not allow satanic doors of opportunity to be opened in their life.

I. Satan is a relentless Opportunist.

II. He carefully monitors the Christian's ability to counter his attacks.

III. A methodical dismantling of fellowshipping is part of his plan.

IV. Nobody understands me better than me syndrome is another ploy.

V. Self-Exaltation on your part, works in the devil's favor.

VI. Imbalanced relationship with worldly people is spiritually dangerous.

VII. Loss of love for the work of ministry open wrong doors.

VIII. Greed is a satanic seed.

IX. He chokes out the Word of God with philosophical idealisms.

Summary:

We are warned to resist the devil **(James 4:7)**, because giving place to the devil is a sure way for Satan to work his traps, strategies and tactics. This dispensation consists of many avenues through which Satan will try to defeat the men and women of God. We must never give him an opportunity to do so.

Lesson 5:

Spiritual Counter-Terrorism!

Scripture Text:
St. John 10:10; I Timothy 6:12

The practice in which militaries, governments and police departments adopt tactics, techniques, and strategies to attack terrorist threats and/or acts, both real and imputed is called **Counter-terrorism**. This approach includes both the detection of potential acts and anything related.

To select the most effective action against terrorism there is a need to understand the source, motivation, methods of preparation and tactics of the terrorist. In a continued effort to alert the people of God to be wise to the devices of Satan; **(II Cor. 2:11),** I strongly suggest these following acts of preparation: Pre-emptive neutralization known as Prayer should be in place. Be knowledgeable and discerning of potential threats.

I. Know the weapons of our warfare. **(II Cor. 10:4)**

II. Stay abreast to old tricks dressed up to deceive you.

III. Campaign to teach fellow Christians how to fight effectively.

IV. Keep your Love for God fresh.

V. Be open to receive the teachings of good leadership.

VI. Hunger and thirst after righteousness. **(St. Matt. 5:6)**

VII. Be willing to pay the ultimate price if necessary. **(Phil. 1:21)**

VIII. Don't allow the false sense of security to deceive you.

Summary:

At the heart of effective Spiritual Counter-Terrorism dwells knowledge and good understanding. We have read and seen the damaging results and effects of spiritual ignorance throughout history. As a called people of God it is far past our time to outwit and outfight the spiritual terrorist cells that dwells comfortably amongst us in this generation. We, **being more than conquerors**; must boldly fight the good fight of faith! **(Romans 8:37; II Tim. 4:7)**

Series 6:

The Future of Your Family

Lesson 1:

The Future of Your Family Series

(Building A Vision For Your Family's Future)

If my people, which are called by my name, shall humble themselves, and pray, and seek my face, and turn from their wicked ways; then will I hear from heaven, and will forgive their sin, and will heal their land.

(II Chronicles 7:14)

Problems for the Family

Here are a few examples of America's family crisis in action:

- 100,000 of America's children are in prisons.
- 40 percent of children live in broken homes.
- 6.5 percent between the ages of seven and eleven have already received psychiatric help.
- The average age of beginning smoking has dropped from 14 to10.
- One million unmarried girls between the ages of 12 and 17 will get pregnant (This figure doesn't even count those who will have abortions).
- One in five children uses drugs twice a week.
- Ten million minors are infected with sexually transmitted diseases.

The concept of leaving a legacy may be unfamiliar to many people. Some understand leaving an inheritance but are not thinking much about leaving their kids with a legacy that reminds them of who they are, what is important in life, and what is their purpose.

Considering your legacy cuts against the grain in our selfish age .It requires pursuing personal spiritual growth, developing a godly family, and reaching out to others in the name of Jesus to change the world. **(Deuteronomy 5:29)**

I. A Vision generates happiness now & later in the life of your family. **(Psalms 23:6; Psalms 128:1-6; Proverbs 29:18)**

II. Share with your family the testimonies of God's goodness. **(Deut. 6:17-18; Psalms 23:6; Psalms 84:10-12; Prov. 8:21)**

III. Extend to others godly advice to exercise in their family. **(Matt. 5:41-48; Deuteronomy 29:9-18)**

Summary:

For other foundation can no man lay than that is laid, which is Jesus Christ. **(I Cor. 3:11)**

If your foundational values are not clear, it will be difficult for you to decide these issues:

- How big the house you will live in or what kind of car you will drive.
- How much money you will make-in a one-or two-career home.
- How much money you will give to charities.
- How high you will climb the corporate ladder.
- How many extra hours a week you will work that will rob you of family time.
- How involved you will be in a local church.

Jesus made a number of points that definitely guide us in answering these questions as we seek to clarify our values. Here are just two:

I. For what is a man profited, if he shall gain the whole world, and lose his own soul? Or what shall a man give in exchange for his soul? **(St. Matt. 16:26) KJV**

II. Therefore take no thought, saying, what shall we eat? Or, what shall we drink? Or, where-withal shall we be clothed? ..... But seek ye first the kingdom of God, and His righteousness; and all these things shall be added unto you. **(St. Matt. 6:31-33)**

Lesson 2:

The Future of Your Family

God has a future for the family. But it won't go well for today's families- and especially for today's children- unless we make some radical changes to bring us back to the principles of God's Word.

God gives us principles and practical strategies for raising families honoring to Him. There are three basic principles Moses teaches us in the sixth chapter of Deuteronomy.

I. The Promise of a Future **(Deut. 6:1-2)**

God promises a future for three generations of the family. The promise begins with the parents and continues with the children and grandchildren.

II. The Foundation for the Family **(Deut. 6:4-5)**

The foundation for the family is a love for God. That may sound simplistic, but it's true. The strength of the love parents have for God is the foundation for the family.

III. The Formula for the Family **(Deut. 6:6-7)**

Parents have the responsibility to transmit their faith to their children. It's not the preacher's job. It's not the Sunday school teacher's job, IT'S THE PARENT'S JOB!!!

Summary:

"Oh that there were such a heart in them, that they would fear me, and keep all my commandments always, that it might be well with them, and with their children forever". **(Deut. 5:29)**

Lesson 3:

Train Your Children Spiritually

I. **Teach convincingly.**
"These words, which I command thee this day, shall be in thine heart" **(Deuteronomy 6:6)**

II. **Teach creatively.**
"Thou shalt teach them diligently unto thy children, and shalt talk of them when thou sittest in thine house, and when thou walkest by the way, and when thou liest down, and when thou risest up" **(Deuteronomy 6:7)** Wise parents and grandparents find countless ways daily to apply the Word of God.

III. **Teach consistently.**
"Teach them diligently unto thy children …." **(Deuteronomy 6:7)**

The prophet Isaiah gave a method for teaching God's truth: "Precept must be upon precept, line upon line, here a little and there a little" **(Isaiah 28:10)**

IV. **Teach conversationally.**
"Thou …shalt talk of them …" **(Deuteronomy 6:7)** God calls us not merely to recite His instructions but to talk of them.

V. **Teach conspicuously.**
"And thou shalt bind them for a sign upon thine hand, and they shall be as frontlets between thine eyes…." **(Deuteronomy 6:8)**

To teach children conspicuously, our houses should have Scriptural mottos, pictures, and other furnishings that remind our children of **Jesus**.

A. In your own words, describe how important it is for children to see an authentic faith in their parents. List some ways you might improve the testimony of your own witness to your children.

B. What principles do you glean about family life from the following passages?

(Genesis 18:17-19)

(Deuteronomy 4:9)

(Proverbs 3:11- 12)

(Proverbs 22:6)

(Ephesians 5:21-6:4)

What are some practical ways to apply these principles in your own family?

____

____

____

____

____

____

Lesson 4:

Resolving Conflicts in Marriage

Conflict is normal and natural in the development of relationships especially in marriage, where two unique individuals enter into an intimate union. In marriage conflicts arise because husbands and wives have different opinions, values, philosophies, and methods. The art of resolving conflicts is a key to keeping a marriage healthy. It is a measure of maturity and part of the lifelong process of "two becoming one." Resolving conflict requires forgiveness. **(Gen. 2:24 ; Matt. 5:23-24; 6:14-15; 18:15-18;Eph. 4:26-32)**

Below are four **"don'ts"** in resolving marital conflicts.

I. Don't refuse to be the first to give in.

II. Don't keep bringing it up and not allowing the conflict to end.

III. Don't attack the person rather than the conflict (which amounts to character assassination).

IV. Don't walk out. Resolve the conflict in its prime.

Summary:

Conflict in marriage may be developmental or it may be devastating; depending on how it is handled. Make resolving the conflict a priority. Don't let anything interfere with resolving it.

Lesson 5:

Dollars and Sense - Managing the Money

Credit card debt, keeping up with the neighbors, separate incomes, separate accounts, "my money" and "your money" instead of **our money** – these are all warning signs for a marriage headed for financial conflict. The solution? Use God's principles to manage money in marriage.

I. God is interested in how you spend your money.

II. God is interested in how you save your money.

III. God is interested in how we share our money.

Some Christians struggle with the concept that God is the source and owner of all our money. That is true simply because God is the source and owner of everything – including money! The scriptures could not be more clear on this point **(Leviticus 25:23; Deuteronomy 8:18; Psalm 24:1; 50:10; Proverbs 10:22; Ezekiel 18:4; Haggai 2:8; I Cor.6:19-20).**

If God is the owner that makes us His stewards or managers. What He gives us to use in our lives on this earth really belongs to Him and we are to use it for His glory.

After everything Job went through losing all of his material possessions and family, he makes an amazing statement about money. **(Job 31:24-25, 28)**

Application/Quiz

Read (Matthew 6:19-24)

I. What does Jesus say not to do regarding financial Resources? (**verse 19**)

II. What is He illustrating about the temporal nature of "things" by citing rust, moths, and thieves? (**verse 19**)

III. What kind of investment protects material wealth from the corruption of this earth? (**verse 20**)

IV. Is it fair to make a judgment about a person's heart based on where and how he invests his treasure? Why or why not? (**verse 21**)

V. WHAT does the key word "also" suggest about the connection between treasure and heart? (**verse 21**)

VI. What is the conclusion Jesus draws in **(verse 24)** about the inseparability of God, money, and the believer?

Lesson 6:

Coping with the Loss of a Family Member

Sometimes disappointment or serious illness shatters the hopes of a household. A tragic accident or untimely death smashes ruthlessly into the home. Hearts are aching and need the ministry of comfort and understanding. True comfort comes when we think things through in the light of the eternal purposes of God for each of us. **(Isaiah 57:1; Romans 14:8)**

I. You can face death without fear. **(Ps.23:4 ; Phil.1:21)**

II. Those who die in the Lord are blessed. **(Rev.13:14; II Corinthians 5:6-8)**

III. There will be a new heaven and a new earth in which there will be no more suffering or sorrowing. **(Rev. 21:1-4)**

IV. Christians are guaranteed an inheritance that can never be destroyed. **(I Peter 1:3-9)**

V. Jesus' resurrection guarantees ours. **(I Corinthians 15:20-23)**

Summary:

Find rest in God alone. Trust in Him at all times under any and all circumstances. **(Psalms 62:5-8)**

Lesson 7:

Gathering of the Family – It's A Celebration

Unfortunately, many families are not able to get together for an enjoyable time of celebration. The tie that binds seem to have little or no effect whatsoever on the need for the family to unite. Busy schedules and selfish agendas cause catastrophic proportions in any chance of a peaceful family gathering. Only when it's too late to rectify this mistake does some realize the importance of the gathering of the family. The "**gathering of the family**" is not a time for the rebirth of arguments or fights due to past discrepancies. It's a time of celebration of your life and the life of your God given family. **(Genesis 10:5)**

I. There are special times when families should gather to celebrate each other. **(Lev. 25:10, 41; Judges 21:24)**

II. God calls for us to remember our family inheritance. **(Genesis 27:7-11)**

III. The fellow-ship of family gatherings aid in strengthening their love for each other. **(Ezekiel 39:28; Matt. 12:25)**

Summary:

God has ordained the family as the foundational institution of human society; it is the starting point of all social, economic, and religious activity.

Series 7:

Managing Your Anger

Lesson 1:

Managing Your Anger Survey

Scripture Text:
Eph. 4:26-32; Prov. 15:1; James 1:19

The first step toward recovering from anger related problems is identifying its various manifestations and recognizing its many faces. Can you identify any of these in your life?

____ Impatience comes over me more frequently than I would like.

____ I nurture critical thoughts quite easily.

____ When I am displeased I shut down or withdraw myself.

____ I feel frustrated when I see someone else having fewer struggles than I do.

____ I walk in another direction to avoid someone I do not like.

____ When discussing controversial topics I raise my voice.

____ I have a hard time accepting someone who refuses to admit his or her weaknesses

____ When I talk about my irritations I don't really want to hear an opposite point of view.

____ I do not easily forget when someone does me wrong.

____ Sometimes my discouragement makes me want to quit.

____ Sometimes I speak slanderously about a person, not really caring how it may harm his or her reputation.

____ I may act kindly on the outside while feeling frustrated on the inside.

____ At times I struggle with moods of depression or discouragement.

____ I have been known to take an "I don't care" attitude toward the needs of others.

Thought:

Be not hasty in thy spirit to be angry; for anger rest in the bosom of fools. **(Ecclesiastes 7:9)**

Lesson 2:

Managing Your Anger

Scripture Text:
Num. 14:18; Jas. 1:20; I Tim. 2:8; Eph. 4:31; Nahum 1:3

Once you have learned to identify anger and understand its meaning, you can then learn to distinguish right and wrong ways of managing it. Although you may not always like the presence of your anger, you can make choices about how you handle it. No two people are exactly alike in managing their anger. Temperaments and circumstances differ widely. There are five general choices that can be made when anger arises:

I. **Suppressing Anger:**

When an anger-producing circumstance occurs, the individual put on a good front and pretend to feel no tension at all.

II. **Open Aggression:**

This category of anger includes explosiveness, ragc, intimidation, blame, criticism, griping and sarcasm.

III. **Passive Aggression:**

Like open aggression, this anger involves preserving personal worth, needs, and convictions at someone else's expense. It is accomplished in a quieter manner, causing less personal vulnerability.

IV. **Assertiveness:**

If anger is defined as preserving personal worth, needs, and convictions, then assertive anger means this preservation is accomplished while considering the needs and feelings of others. It represents a mark of personal maturity and stability.

V. **Dropping it:**

Of the choices involving anger the most difficult one is to let it go. This option includes tolerance of differences as well as choosing to forgive.

Summary:

Often, people have trouble handling their anger with good choices because they have not resolved the tensions linked to their environments.

Lesson 3:

(Self-Inflicted Anger)

When most people try to determine the reasons for their anger, they point to external pressures. For example, my spouse is uncooperative. My parents neglected basic needs. My job is stressful. My friends don't know how to relate to me. My children are rebellious. Problems like these certainly create anger, but they do not tell the whole story. A lot of anger is due to self-inflicted wounds. Though the environment may in fact present difficulties, we all have free will to manage our adult lives. Some of us create our own anger by making poisonous choices. A few poisonous choices are listed below.

I. **Compromising Your Morals. (Matt. 7:13)**

Too many people perpetuate their anger by compromising their morals to gain acceptance. In the short term, some satisfaction is felt. But over the long term immorality and emotional turmoil go hand in hand. **(Pr. 14:12)**

II. **Overworking Yourself for Financial Gain.**

When people are consumed by work and busyness they typically describe themselves as stressed. Stress has been used as such a vague, catchall term it deflects us from recognizing the anger that is a part of it. Overworked, stressful people are angry. **(Matt. 16:26)**

III. **Poor Health Habits.**

Some poor health habits possibly related to self-inflicted anger are such things as overeating, smoking, poor exercise, poor hygiene and lack of sleep. Such habits also cause us to focus on worries that might otherwise be avoided. **(3 John:2)**

Summary:

Anger management is ultimately linked to spiritual stability. When we maintain a daily relationship with God, our problems are less overwhelming. Being at peace with God empowers us to confidently combat worldly imperfections.

Self-Inflicted Anger Survey

Check the following statements that apply to you to help decide if pride or morality problems play a role in your anger buildup.

____ My friends are able to entice me toward activities I should probably avoid.

____ I am entertained by crude humor.

____ I cling to lustful thoughts and fantasies.

____ Cutting corners in my responsibilities is easier now than it was five years ago.

____ Going to church is more of a ritual than a truly purposeful experience.

____ I often put on a false front, hoping to create a good impression.

____ I have a great desire to appear successful.

____ There have been times when I have passed along negative rumors about a successful person.

____ I spend too much money on things such as clothes or cars to the extent that I put myself in financial jeopardy.

____ I keep score of my own gains in comparison to the gains of friends and family.

Lesson 4:

Lingering Anger

Prov. 6:27; Eccl. 7:9; Matt. 5:23-24; Num. 15:30-31

When we cling to anger in spite of potentially helpful knowledge and insights, it is usually due to an intricate system of rationalizations that perpetuate anger. Change is difficult. It requires persistent effort and a stubborn willingness to restructure the thoughts and perceptions that guide us. By hiding behind rationalizations we shun personal responsibility. We sometimes choose to think, "My anger is the result of someone else's problems". Below are a few rationalizations that cause lingering anger.

My past is too painful.

To get beyond a painful past we must humbly acknowledge our inability to control others, particularly when the experiences are irretrievable.

Forgiveness is too good.

When the person to be forgiven has done nothing to deserve forgiveness you cling to the anger because forgiveness seems to let others off the hook too easily.

Why should I try when no one else does?

When we require fairness as a prerequisite for anger management, we ask for trouble.

Example: You want to resolve the problem but the other person is being stubborn, not willing to make amends.

Anger is a familiar habit.

Just as we can get hooked on alcohol or food or materialism, we can become hooked on anger. You go back to it again and again not particularly because you like it, but because it is a familiar part of your routine.

Summary:

Avoid the temptation to rationalize your anger; assume full responsibility for who you are. Anger reduction is much easier when everyone involved makes equal effort toward harmony. But that's not likely in many cases.

You can determine if you are rationalizing your anger by asking the following questions:

I. Do I express my anger aggressively in spite of my good intentions to be properly assertive?

II. Are my episodes of inappropriate anger a repeat of earlier, similar incidents?

III. Do I have a feeling the world owes me more than it is willing to give?

IV. Do I blame God for my problems, cynically questioning why He won't spare me from my miseries?

V. Have I become insensitive to the way my anger affects the well-being of other people?

VI. Have I given up hope that I can be a consistently balanced person?

Be as honest as you can with yourself. What excuses do you hide behind to justify your ongoing unhealthy anger?

1.____

____

____

2. ____

____

____

3. ____

____

____

Be not hasty in thy spirit to be angry; for anger rest in the bosom of fools.

Eccl.7:9

Lesson 5:

Be Accountable

No one can claim immunity from emotional trauma. Yet many people like to pretend they have no struggles. This only increases their tendency toward stress (which spawns anger) and aggravate relational tensions. Let's be honest with each other. When you feel angry or depressed or tense, talk about it. Be accountable for your ongoing growth and open about your anger management. **(Rom. 14:12)**

I. Set goals to become more relational. **(Heb. 12:14-17)**

To promote a more rewarding and responsible manner of relating, the causes of your anger must be identified. Persistent anger inhibits success in relationships because an angry person repels others.

II. Make amends with those you have wronged. **(Rom. 13:7-8)**

To truly find balance we must be willing to make amends with those who have been hurt by our past behavior and attitudes. Families have collapsed because of unresolved anger. Business partnerships, friendships, and church fellowships have suffered because people cling too powerfully to their anger.

III. Choose to be positive in your communication. **(I Cor. 15:33-34)**

Once you understand the meaning and underlying causes of your anger you can formulate goals that will reflect a change of heart. You can deliberately set out to establish a reputation as someone who is caring rather than full of grudges.

Summary:

An inevitable by-product of misguided anger is damaged relationships and the highest aim in living is to know how to connect voluntarily with others in God's love.

To determine if you lean toward addictive anger tendencies, check the following items that apply to you.

__ Sometimes my angry response far exceeds the importance of the conflict at hand.

__ Inwardly I direct myself to stop my angry behavior, but it continues in spite of my self-instructions.

__ At times I experience a "free floating" anger, strong emotion that is not tied to any particular event.

__ I can experience rapid mood changes; one moment I'm fine, then suddenly I become perturbed.

__ Others have told me they're never quite sure how I will respond to a sensitive topic.

__ Rather than brewing over minor problems, I intend to give them less attention.

__ I try to develop a greater reputation as an encouraging person.

__ I have a history of broken relationships or of few close relationships.

__ I don't seem to learn from past mistakes as well as I should.

Respond to the following sentences:

When I am caught in anger my primary goal seems to be____

As I choose to moderate my anger, my new goal will be to ____

*Every man that strives for the mastery is temperate in all things *
(I Cor.9:25a)

Series 8:

Growing Toward Spiritual Maturity!

Lesson 1:

The House of God!!!

Scripture Text:
I Kings 5:5; I Chron. 22:19; Psalms 122:1

By Divine design we have been given the charge to build up the House of God. It is with great disappointment that many disregard this Biblical order. The place of worship has been categorized and treated as an optional pit stop for temporary appeasement. How we enter and what we do when attending the place of worship is vitally important to God. If our Heavenly Father took time to say, build it; we should certainly take time to not only attend, but to beautify it with praise and worship. God is the Perfect Host that enjoys the presence of His people.

The House of God serves our human necessities in many ways:

I. The house of God serves as a place of refuge.

II. The house of God is the place where the Spirit of God resides.

III. The house of God is a meeting place of encouragement.

IV. The house of God is sacred grounds.

V. The house of God is a physical place where believers come for replenishment.

VI. The house of God serves as a spiritual hospital to those who are sin sick.

VII. The house of God serves as a school of higher learning.

VIII. The house of God serves as a diner to those hungry for truth.

IX. The house of God serves as a well for those thirsty for righteousness.

X. The house of God is the physical storehouse for the work of evangelism.

XI. The house of God is where believers go to praise and worship The Father.

XII. The house of God is the birthing ground for new converts and ministries.

Summary:

Within the walls of the house of God is a peace that the woes of this world cannot penetrate. There is also a certain ambience and joy that illuminates the atmosphere. Anyone that forsakes the assembling of himself with the body of Christ (within the house of God) is doing himself a great injustice. **(Hebrews 10:24-25)**

Lesson 2:

Information and Illumination

(Applying Scriptural Knowledge to Everyday Life)

Scripture Text:
St. Matthew 5:14-16; Isaiah 42:6; 49:6; 60:3

One of our biggest setbacks in Christendom is the inability to illuminate our new life effectively. We have certain knowledge of scriptures but may not know how to properly exercise that knowledge. The information of Scripture carries enough power to ignite the ministry in any born again, Holy Ghost filled believer. We sometimes make the mistake of assuming God will through transcendence move us into our area of ministering. Not everyone will have a Phillip experience.

Definitions: Information - knowledge obtained from investigation, study, or instruction.

Illumination - an observable property and effect of light.

In the study of the "Sermon on the Mount", Jesus not only used salt as a metaphor, but He also used light. It should be understood that salt is what's in you, while light is what others should see coming out of you. As long as you have the "Light" (which is generated by the Holy Ghost and by the power of God's Word) people will see a difference in you. They will see a difference that clearly identifies you as a true Christian and a true child of God. Light is an important ingredient in the character of anyone that is on a mission to win souls for the Kingdom of God. Here are five facts about a Christian's Light:

I. Your Light chases away darkness (sin).

II. Your Light reveals both what's on the inside and outside of you.

III. Your Light is a reflection of who God is and who you are.

IV. Your Light enhances spiritual insight (whether you are the observer or the one being observed).

V. Your Light brightens even more as you grow in relation to God.

Summary:

Light is linked with instruction **(Psalms 119:105,130)**, truth **(Ps. 43:3),** good **(Isa. 5:20**), salvation **(Ps. 49:6)**, life **(Job 33:28, 30),** peace **(Isa. 45:7),** rejoicing **(Ps.97:11**), covenant **(Isa. 42:6),** justice and righteousness **(Isa. 59:9)**, God's presence and favor **(Ps.89:15)**.

Lesson 3:

Rekindle Your Faith!!!

Scripture Text.:
St. Matt. 9:29; Heb. 10:38; Heb. 11:1

Sometimes the faith of an individual is worn thin by the everyday trials of life. The ups and downs of everyday living, the opposition of enemy attacks and the betrayal of those people once trusted can cause ones faith to wilt. It is quite essential for Christians to rekindle their faith each and every day. Below are essential and helpful ways of rekindling your faith:

I. Have true love for God. **(St. John 14:21)**

II. Stay prayerful regardless of your circumstances. **(I Thess. 5:17)**

III. Study the Word of God relentlessly. **(II Timothy 2:15)**

IV. Bond with other dedicated and strong Christians. **(Hebrews 13:3)**

V. Witness to others regarding your relationship with Christ. **(Hebrews 12:1)**

VI. Attend church regularly - Praise and Worship services. **(Heb. 10:24-25)**

VII. Avoid negative talk and conversations. **(I Cor. 15:33)**

VIII. Develop a heart for true worship. **(St. John 4:24)**

IX. Be filled with the Holy-Ghost and stay on fire. **(St. Matt. 3:11; Acts 1:8)**

Summary:

We face enough challenges in life to verify the necessity for us to keep our faith on fire. Sometimes the flames of our faith seem dim and questionable. Thanks be to God our faith can be rekindled through careful attention and godly sincerity. Waste no time in rekindling your faith, for faith is your lifeline that revitalizes your strength to walk with God.

Lesson 4:

How Much Time Are You Giving God In Corporate Worship?

Scripture Text:
II Chronicles 7:14; Eccl. 3:1; Hosea 4:6-7

There are 168 hours in a week and only 12 hours of this time is set aside for corporate worship. I took a few minutes of my time to calculate an approximate use of one's time in the course of a week. These are my approximations (for Emmanuel Temple Church Of God - assuming two hours as the average duration of corporate worship).

Sunday- School – 2 hours

Sunday Morning Worship – 2 hours

Wed. Night Bible Study – 2 hours

Friday Night Worship – 2 hours

Wed.-Noonday Prayer, Wed.-Night Hour of Power

Prayer, Thurs. - Intercessory Prayer & Sat. Morning (11am) Prayer – (Totaling 4 hours of Corporate Prayer per week).

The total amount of Corporate Worship equals 12 hours.

These totals are based on the assumption that an individual attends all of the above services each week. (An unlikely assumption for too many).

168 hours total per week

minus - 8 hours of Corporate Worship

minus - 4 hours of Corporate Prayer

minus - 40 hours of work or school per week

minus - 56 hours of sleep (8hrs per night)

That leaves **<u>60 hours</u>** of the week for shopping, playing and anything else you choose to do with the time that **God has given you. Surely we can give God more than an occasional two hours per Sunday!!!**

Lesson 5:

Risk and Reward

Living your life according to the precepts of God is a no-risk route to success in this life and the next. And four key passages of Scripture explain why. I encourage you to read and meditate on each as you contemplate how God defines success.

(Joshua 1:6-9)
Meditating on God's Word day and night, being careful to do everything written in it, will bring prosperity and success. Strength and courage will characterize you as you walk through this world.

(Psalm 1)
Delighting in "the law of the Lord," meditating on it day and night, will cause you to be fruitful and prosperous. You will avoid the counsel of the ungodly, the path of the sinful, and the seat of the scornful.

(Matthew 5:3-12)
These "beatitudes," as they have been called, characterize the man or woman who is blessed and happy in this life. Humility, mourning, being meek, hungering for righteousness, showing mercy, purity, making peace, suffering for Jesus – these are what bring blessing(success) in God's sight.

(Philippians 3:7-14)
Leaving behind the world's fame and power, Paul found success in pressing forward toward making Jesus Christ his all in all.

Summary:

Whether your wealth and fame spread around the block or around the world, stay successful in God's sight by making Him the focus of it all.

Lesson 6:

The Subtlety of Spiritual Death

Scripture Test:
Hosea 4:6-7

The misconception of freedom of choice has caused many Christians to wither and die a subtle spiritual death. People are told; it's okay to be what you want to be and say what you want to say, whenever, where-ever and how-ever you desire. Some live their Christian lives very sketchy; never yielding godly fruit. Their spiritual diagnosis reveals non-edifying and non-productive internal damages- both resulting in spiritual death. Here are some applicable preventive maintenance check points for avoiding the subtlety of spiritual death.

I. Because the majority is doing it, doesn't mean it's right. **(I Thess. 5:21- 22)**

II. You are held accountable for your own actions. **(Rom. 14:12)**

III. Ask such questions as; "What does the Word of God say about it"? **(II Tim. 2:15 ; John 5:39-42)**

IV. Protect your inner man by feeding on the Word daily. **(Acts 17:10-12)**

V. Attend Church regularly, not occasionally. **(Heb. 10:24-25)**

VI. Don't allow mishaps to squash your faith in God. **(Luke 22:32)**

VII. Have both a strong personal and corporate prayer life. **(Jas. 5:16; I Thess. 5:17; Acts 12:5)**

Summary:

"Satan hath desired to have you that he may sift you as wheat". **(St. Luke 22:31)**

Lesson 7:

God Fulfills His Promises

Scripture Text:
II Chron. 6:12-17; Luke 24:44-49

People have been known to make promises they didn't keep. When people do keep promises, especially to us personally, it makes us trust them more. The same is true for God. The scriptures declare that God has kept every promise He ever made and continues to do so. But what about promises we make to God?

I. God's fulfilling of promises is birthed by His true love for mankind.

II. Our promises to God should be birthed by our true love for God.

III. Our obedience to the Word of God strengthens our anticipation for promise fulfillment.

IV. **Jesus Christ** is the affirmation of God's **kept** promises past, present and future.

Summary:

We are grateful for promises God has kept in times past and our obedience through faith anticipate God keeping His promises in the future.

Lesson 8:

Forget Not His Benefits

Scripture Text:
Psalms 103: 2-5

We often (and appropriately) focus on the difficulties that may face us in our Christian walk. However, it's equally important to spend time reflecting on the benefits that we have in the Lord. David reminds us in Psalm 103 not to forget His benefits:

Definition: Benefits – useful aid; help, advantage

I. He forgives your sins (**3a**).

II. He heals your diseases (**3b**).

III. He redeems your life from destruction (**4a**).

IV. He crowns you with grace and mercy (**4b**).

V. He satisfies you with Good Things (**5a**)

VI. He renews your strength (**5b**).

Summary:

Bless the Lord, O my soul, and forget not all His benefits.
(Psalm 103:2)

Lesson 9:

Shall We Continue in Sin? God Forbid!

Scripture Text:
Romans 6:1-14

The silent and sometimes boisterous approach of some is: "Keep doing what you've always done", "God understands", "Don't feel convicted or guilty about those secret sins you commit", "Ignore the warnings of the preacher, he'll soon move on to other lessons of interest".

This line of thinking has poisoned the minds of many so-called Christians far too long. It is time for the real people of God to step forward and proclaim the heavenly standards of holy living. We must never substitute humanism, pragmatism or any other ism in place of obedience to the Word of God.

The purpose of this lesson outline is to expose the subtle abode of sin in the lives of people that once opposed even the slightest resemblance or indication of sin. Once we are knowledgeable of sinful behavior in our lives, we should no longer continue therein.

I. If you are sneaking due to uncertainty, you probably need to stop.

II. If it's obviously wrong, you should definitely stop. **(I Thess. 5:22-23)**

III. Sin is very convincing that it's a necessity.

IV. Sin will rob you of logical and godly reasoning.

V. Sin has lasting repercussions.

VI. The ending result of sin is spiritual death. **(Romans 6:23)**

Summary:

Good understanding give favor: but the way of transgressors is hard.

(Proverb 13:15)

Lesson 10:

Four Reasons to Trust God with Daily Needs

Scripture Text:
Deuteronomy 1:19-33

Many of us are intellectually persuaded of the truthfulness of Christianity and have personally trusted Christ as Savior. Regretfully, on a daily basis, we struggle with trusting God with everyday needs. In Deuteronomy 1, Moses recounted the story of the twelve spies **(Numbers 13-14)** and gave four reasons to trust God with our burdens.

I. We should trust God because of His Commands. **(v.21).** "Do not fear or be discouraged **(v.29).**" "Do not be terrified or afraid." God has commanded us to trust Him.

II. We should trust God because of His Promises **(v.30).** "The Lord your God, who goes before you, He will fight for you." The battle is the Lord's, and He promises we will be more than conquerors through Him who loved us.

III. We should trust God because of His Past Faithfulness. **(v.31).** "In the wilderness …you saw how the Lord your God carried you, as a man carries his son."

IV. We should trust God because of His Personalized Care. **(vv. 32-33).**"Your God… went in the way before you to search out a place for you to pitch your tents, to show you the way you should go."

Summary:

Instead of fretting about it, try faith-ing it. Trust God with your daily cares.

Lesson 11:

Never Mind That!

Scripture Text:
II Timothy 1:7; Romans 8:5-8

The phrase, "Never mind that!" is one of the most well-known phrases for excusing oneself from confusing or troubling thoughts. This phrase can also be a deathtrap for any Christian willing to ignore the subtle trickery of the devil, our enemy.

Sometimes the enemy will try to influence you to think stinking thoughts in regards to other Christians. That Old Deceiver will even try to lead you to believe that God no longer cares for you. With this thought in mind we can see why some Christians, if not prayerful, will self-destruct. It would benefit any purpose driven Christian to be very selective and protective of what is processed in their thought life. Be on guard because the battle for your soul begins in your mind. Consider these points before yielding:

I. We mustn't disregard the subtlety of stinking thinking.

II. We should analyze the thought and identify the origin.

III. When it is evident that God is not glorified, abandon the thought.

IV. Occupy your mind/heart with the Holy Scriptures.

V. Learn to discern the oncoming of good thoughts versus bad.

VI. Avoid filthy literature; when you read it you store it subconsciously.

VII. Avoid filthy jokes.

VIII. Avoid filthy shows or movies (i.e., television, dvd, theatre, plays etc.).

IX. Avoid negative conversations (i.e., telephone calls, e-mail, texting etc.).

X. Be led by the Spirit of God, not selfish ambitions. **(Romans 8:14)**

Summary:

You will guard him and keep him in perfect and constant peace whose mind (both its inclination and its character) is stayed on You, because he commits himself to You, leans on You, and hopes confidently in You. **(Isaiah 26:3)** AMP

Lesson 12:

How You Can Be Healed!!!

God has a lot of ways to heal us based on the redemptive plan of Christ. It is something Jesus paid for something He suffered for. His desire for you to be healed and walk in divine health is the reason He went through so much pain and suffering. He has made healing available to you through many avenues.

I. Healing through the laying on of hands. **(Luke 4:40).**

   A. Everyone who came to Jesus got healed. No exceptions.

II. Healing through deliverance. **(Matthew 8:16; Luke 8:2).**

   A. Some people need deliverance from the spirit of infirmities.

III. Healing through breaking curses. **(Galatians 3:13).**

   A. People are plagued with generational infirmities such as diabetes, high blood pressure, certain heart conditions and more.

IV. Healing through anointing oil. **(Mark 6:13; Isaiah 10:27)**

   A. Anointing oil represents the Spirit of God and the anointing.

V. Healing through faith. **(Mark 11:23)**

   A. (Keep your heart free from doubt and unbelief) Grow up in faith.

VI. Healing through virtue or touch. **(Mark 5:29-30; Luke 6:19; Matt. 14:36).**

A. Jesus' virtue can be in you if you pray and fast.

VII. Healing through the Word. **(Psalms 107:20; 118:17)**

A. Trust God because His Word will accomplish in you all that He intends.

VIII. Healing through prayer. **(Matt.21:22; James 5:16)**

A. "All things" (KJV) includes healing.

Summary:

The more people hear and are taught about healing, the greater will be their capacity to put a demand on it.

Lesson 13:

SIN
(Self-Inflicted Nonsense)

Sin is defined as any act regarded as such a transgression, especially a willful or deliberate violation of some religious or moral principle. Within the confines of Christianity, all unrighteousness is sin. **(I John 5:17)**

One of the biggest mistakes of some people is to believe that God is going to overlook their wrongs. We must not forget; it is not within the nature of God to commune with anyone that regards iniquity in their heart. **(Psalms 66:18)** The purpose of this lesson is to reveal the fact that sin is nothing more than self-inflicting nonsense, especially when our behavior contrasts the laws of our Holy God.

I. Sin may be acts or deeds. **(Jude 15)**

II. Sin is the omission of proper behavior. **(James 4:17)**

III. Sin is of the devil. **(I John 3:8)**

IV. The penalty for un-forgiven sins is death. **(Romans 6:23)**

V. Sin must be repented of. **(Luke 13:3; Acts 2:38)**

VI. The blood of Jesus provides atonement for sin. **(I John 1:7)**

VII. Believers can enjoy spiritual victory over sin by walking in the Spirit. **(Galatians 5:16; Romans 6:14)**

Summary:

But your iniquities have separated between you and your God, and your sins have hid his face from you, that he will not hear. **(Isaiah 59:2).**

Lesson 14:

"The Marks of Jesus"

"From henceforth let no man trouble me: for I bear in my body the marks of the Lord Jesus." **(Galatians 6:17)** Extra biblical sources reveal that when Paul wrote these words, the branding iron was inflicted not only on animals, but also on humans, leaving marks on the flesh that could never be removed.

At least three classes of individuals bore scars of this kind (1) slaves who were owned by their masters;(2) soldiers who branded themselves with the name of their commanding general as a token of their wholehearted dedication, and (3) devotees who were attached for life to the temple of the deity worshipped there.

Let us observe the lifelong marks of a dedicated Christian:

I. Like the slave, a dedicated Christian bears the mark of ownership of the Master who owns him. **(Romans 1:1; I Cor. 6:19-20)**

II. Like the soldier, a dedicated Christian bears the mark of devotion to the Commander he serves. **(II Cor. 5:15; II Timothy 2:3)**

III. Like the devotee, a dedicated Christian bears the mark of a worshipper of the Lord he adores. **(II Cor. 4:5; Philippians 1:20)**

Summary:

Most likely, Paul is referring to the scars from wounds his persecutors had inflicted on him, scars that were self-evident marks that he belonged to Christ forever.

Lesson 15:

"Characteristics of Our Savior"

I. He is a perfect Savior.

Who never sinned against God or man. **(Matthew 27:3-4; John 18:38; John 19:4, 6; I Peter 2:22)**

II. Who was inwardly as well as outwardly perfect. **(Matthew 17:5; Hebrews 10:5-7; I Peter 1:19)**

III. He is a vicarious(done or suffered by one person on behalf of another or others) Savior.

A. Who bore our guilt upon the cross **(Isaiah 53:6-10; I Peter 2:24)**

B. Who died to save us from our sins **(Romans 4:25; I Peter 3:18)**

IV. He is a justifying Savior.

A. Who is the means by grace of our justification before God. **(Romans 3:24)**

B. Who becomes our righteousness through faith in His redemptive work **(Romans 3:21-23; Romans 5:1; I Corinthians 1:30-31)**

Summary:

We as Christians sometimes get lost in the maze of establishing who we are in the body of Christ. If not careful, we can find ourselves neglecting the important duty of identifying Christ for who He is to us.

Lesson 16:

"Giving Thanks'

Scripture Text:
Acts 16:16-34

Giving thanks to God is one of the most powerful things we can do as believers. He works mightily through the praises of His people.

When we tell the Father how much we love Him and appreciate all He does for us, we acknowledge we are dependent upon His provision and sovereignty. With this attitude of gratitude we allow God to exhibit His maximum impact in our lives.

The question is: How can we keep expressing our gratefulness to God when life becomes challenging and we experience painful trials?

First: In order to have a life characterized by thanksgiving and praise, we must keep our focus on God, rather than our circumstances. **(Psalms 100:1-5)**

Second: When difficult circumstances arise, recall the ways the Lord has helped you in the past. **(Ecclesiastes 12:1-2)**

Third: Consider the consequences of unbelief. **(St. John 3: 16-21)**

Fourth: Enjoy the benefits of thanksgiving. **(Psalms 103:1-5)**

Summary:

Like Paul and Silas, focus on God rather than circumstances. Recall how He has helped you in the past and have faith He will provide for you in the future. Give thanks unto the Lord!

Lesson 17:

God Revealed Himself as Jealous

Scripture Text.:
Exodus 20:1-7; Exodus 34:14

Jealousy! The simple mention of the word stirs unsavory feelings and emotions. It speaks of bitterness, envy, and harshness. It has separated husband from wife, siblings, and choice friends. Its havoc appears in divorce courts, in broken relationships, and in lonely lives.

Consequently, it is almost shocking that the Word of God describes God as jealous! However, God is explicit in this self-revelation of His jealous nature. In His delivery of the Ten Commandments, the Lord expressly stated, "I the Lord thy God am a jealous God". (**Exodus 20:5**).

What does God mean when He says He is "jealous"? Does this mean something different from the human application of that term? What is the righteous framework for His jealousy, and what is our righteous response to it?

I. God is Distinct

A. God's Distinctiveness Allows Him to Be Jealous.

B. God's Distinctiveness Permits No Rivals.

II. God is Jealous

A. God's jealousy is not selfish. It endeavors to protect us from the hurt we will experience if we reject Christ and His rule in our lives.

B. God's jealousy for us is born out of a desire for our best interests and produces guidelines and protections for our spiritual well-being.

Summary:

God is too holy for us to walk with Him while clinging to unrighteous values and desires. **(I Cor. 3:16-17)**

Lesson 18:

"Kingdom Priority"

Scripture Text.:
St. Matthew 6:19, 33; Luke 12:34

The problem in most people's lives is God is not first. He cannot be one amongst many other things. He must be first. First is always first. Putting God first is not a request it is a command. **(Exodus 20:3)**

To many people God is their spare tire. He is sought after only when things go flat in their lives. When there are relationship problems, financial problems or should health issues arise; they suddenly remember to call on God.

The priority of seeking first the Kingdom of God should never get lost in the busyness of life. Living in this world is a demanding experience. Life's demanding experiences must always be met by first priority and that Priority should be to seek first the Kingdom of God and His righteousness. **(St. Matt. 6:33)**

I. Love God above any and everything or any and everybody.

II. God first loved us, it's no strain to love Him back. **(I Jn.4:19)**

III. Love is an action word; we should act upon our love for God in word and deed. **(I Jn.2:3-6;3:23-24;5:2-3; II Jn.6; Rev.22:14)**

IV. The first fruits of everything we say or do should be to God's glory**. (Proverbs 3:9; Colossians 1:18)**

V. God is a jealous God therefore we cannot share our heart with other gods. **(Exodus 20:5;34;14-16)**

Summary:

Jesus made no mistake in pointing out the necessity to seek first the Kingdom of God and His righteousness. There are no substitutes for bountiful blessings, the Lord Himself has spoken!

Lesson 19:

What's Missing in Your Life?

Scripture Text:
St. John 3:16; Jeremiah 20:9

We go through life in search of our purpose and cause for being. We encounter defining moments in our life; we then have moments where we feel stagnant or lost. All of us go through this process or phase at some point in life. The void we experience is the intuition to know that we are missing a vital part of our being. The only one that can fill that void is the Lord Jesus Christ.

Without His being the biggest part of who you are; life is as boring as watching paint dry. You must ask yourself, what's missing? Why am I not enjoying my life to the fullest? The answer lies in the pages of the Bible. God's Holy Word!

I. You are living beneath the privileges/benefits afforded to you in Christ. **(Psalm 103:1-5)**

II. You are missing real joy. **(Nehemiah 8:10)**

III. You are missing genuine happiness. **(Psalms 1:1)**

IV. You are missing true love. **(I Cor.13:1-3)**

V. Your soul is starving for something far greater than material gain. **(St. Matt. 16:26; St. Mark 8:36; St. Luke 9:25)**

Summary:

In this fast pace society we live in, we find ourselves chasing after something we think will fulfill our cravings. When we catch up with it we are disappointed and begin to question the whole purpose of life.

The missing factor in anyone's life that is hungry for real meaning, is a life fulfilled with the loving presence of God. His inclusion in your life eliminates the void and emptiness. Give your life to Jesus and begin to live life the way God intended. Joyously!

Lesson 20:

Stop, Pray, then Wait on God!

Scripture Text:
Isaiah 40:31; I Thess. 5:17

While driving a car you may come upon a stop sign or a stoplight. Of course these two objects are indications that you need to cease from moving forward. Should you decide to ignore the warnings, you run the risk of having an accident. Sometimes one can walk away from such incidents and sometimes one is carried away. This is an analogy used to explain the danger of ignoring the warning signs issued by God. It would be to our advantage to take heed to every message God sends. If it's a preaching, teaching or written message; it deserves your attention and obedience. Stop, Pray for guidance then wait on God for answers.

I. When we pray and wait, we avoid unnecessary pitfalls.

II. We learn the voice of God.

III. We learn to endure.

IV. We learn to become victorious.

V. We discover God's purpose for our life.

VI. We move to a deeper level of praying.

VII. We bring our flesh into subjection to God's Will. **(I Cor.9:27)**

Summary:

Stopping can sometimes be a challenge in itself. Sometimes what we want clashes with what God wants for us. When we stop, pray and wait for God's answer everything works out for our good. **(Romans 8:28)**

Lesson 21:

Balance between Church and Home

The highest calling an individual can receive in this life is the call by God to preach His Word. This call requires the individual to sometimes make drastic sacrifices. Not everyone is willing to make such sacrifices. There has been many times as a preacher that not only I, but the entire family has put our plans on hold in order to fulfill ministerial requirements. Despite all the sacrifices, God has never called me to stop being a husband to my wife or to stop being a father to my children. After all, He is the One that sanctioned families.

Regardless of how busy things may be in our church life, our family never stops being a family. We always endeavor to keep a healthy balance between our home life and our church life.
To the preacher and his/her family, it is in your best interest to maintain balance between church and home. There are times when the enemy will try to use the busyness of church work to methodically dismantle the joy of home life.

I. The Foundation of the family – **(Psalms 127:1a; Joshua 24:15)**

   The base of every preacher's home should be established on godly living. It's so important to know that your calling is God ordained.

II. The Flexibility of the family – **(I Cor. 9:27; Proverbs 11:29; I Tim.3:5)**

   The Golden Gate Bridge in San Francisco, California will sway as much as 20 feet. It maintains its strength because of the two towers that are solidly anchored. Likewise, the preacher's household must be solidly anchored; no matter what is going on in the church.

III. The Fruit of the family-

There are a number of things in life that God has favored man with. One very joyous favor is the blessing of bearing children. Raising children can be challenging, but it also brings character to the family. Most importantly, our children remind us of how patient and loving our Father-God is with us.

Summary:

The foundation, flexibility and fruit of a family are all a part of maintaining a balance between home and church life. It is our prayers that God's blessings will flow within your home and church. **(Psalms 37:23-25)**

Lesson 22:

Are You Purpose Driven?

The condition of our spirituality is greatly dependent upon how deeply we are purpose driven. A number of men and women of God lose purpose and focus and become complacent in a non-productive status. This is only a ploy of Satan to destroy the army of the living God. Should we decide to push beyond the borders set up by the enemy, we will discover a whole new realm of sanctification we never knew existed. We must be purpose driven with an hunger and thirst that only obedience to the will of God will quench.

Definition: Purpose – a result which is desired and kept in mind in performing an action, 2) willpower.

Driven – a cause to work very hard

I. We must be both faithful and effective . **(Psalms 31:22-24)**

II. We must equip ourselves with both spiritual blinders and a bridle. **(St. John 9:39-41; Psalms 32:8-9)**

III. We must be both hungry and thirsty for victorious living. **(St. Matthew 5:6)**

Summary:

It is essential to our lives both spiritually and naturally to have a drive beyond normal expectation. We cannot accomplish anything meaningful in life without such astronomical and purpose driven motives. We are more than conquerors and we should pursue God given goals in that respect. Are you purpose driven?

Lesson 23:

My God vs. My Flesh

(To whom will I listen?)

Scripture Reference:
Galatians 5:16-26; I Corinthians 9:27

Unfortunately for us, we sometimes find ourselves engaged in a struggle between what our flesh craves as opposed to what God wants for us. It should never get to the point where such a scenario becomes so intensified; however, we occasionally lean to the hunger of the flesh. The Spirit of God will never lead us to do something in the flesh that will contrast the written Word of God. When we learn to obey the Spirit of God we will not be so apt to fulfill the lust of our flesh. God has given us the remedy.

I. Our flesh hungers for carnal things, self–satisfying cravings. **(Romans 7:5**, **Romans 8:6)**

II. A Spirit filled person hungers for godly fulfillment. **(Psalm 51:10**, **St. Matt.5:8)**

III. Spending time in prayer will sensitize your obedience to God. (**I Thess. 5:17**, **I Cor. 14:14-15)**

IV. Fasting will discipline the hunger of your flesh. **(St. Matt.17:20-21, St. Matt. 6:16-18)**

Summary:

We should be mindful of the choices we make in life. Sometimes our choices are conflicting with the will of God and will only lead to spiritual degradation.

Lesson 24:

Time Sensitive Living!!!

Scripture Text:
Eccl. 3:1-9;12:1-2

Sometimes we make an assumption that we have more time than needed for us to do God's Will. To come to such an understanding is deceptive and very misleading. God has afforded us a limited time to live our lives and we must be aware of the urgency to live it pleasingly to His Glory. We sometimes receive mail stamped, "Time Sensitive Material".

Our first inclination is to open it so we can find out its contents. Within the pages of the Bible (**B**asic **I**nstructions **B**efore **L**eaving **E**arth) we are given instructions on how to live this "Time Sensitive" life. God has granted us precise time and we must use it wisely.

Below are a few "Time Sensitive" reminders:

I. We are here for a short period of time. **(Psalms 89:47-48)**

II. Hardship touches each of us at some point in life. **(Eccl.9:11-12)**

III. God reminds us of His Love and His Will for us even in our time of rebellion and stubbornness. **(Ezekiel 16:8-14)**

IV. God will restore us and reset us. **(Ps.23:3;Ps.51:10-12)**

V. We all have an expiration date stamped on us. **(II Timothy 4:6, Hebrews 9:27)**

VI. God allows us time to get our houses in order. **(II Kings 20:1-11)**

VII. Every single moment is precious and valuable time. **(II Cor. 6:2)**

Summary:

God, in His wise providence know the frailty of man. He is not requiring of us something difficult and unattainable. He wants our time to center around His Time. He wants our ambitions to be birthed through a hunger to please Him and to always do His will. Jesus is still saying to us, “If you love me, keep my commandments.”

Lesson 25:

Everlasting /Eternal Life

Everlasting Life is defined as life at its best having fellowship with God. This important term in the New Testament is emphasized in the Gospel of John but also appears in the other gospels and in Paul's writings. Eternal Life in the NT eliminates the boundary line of death. Death is still a foe, but the person who has eternal life already experiences the kind of existence that will never end. Yet in this expression, the emphasis is on the quality of life rather than on the unending duration of life.

Everlasting/Eternal Life is:

I. Life imparted by God. **(St. John 3:15-16; St. John 3:36;Romans 6:23)**

II. Transformation and renewal of life. **(Romans 12:1-2; Titus 3:7)**

III. Life fully opened to God and centered in Him. **(Gal.6:7-10; Titus 1:2)**

IV. A constant overcoming of sin and moral evil. **(I Cor.15:58)**

V. The complete removal of moral evil from the person and from the environment of that person. **(Romans 5:17-21)**

Summary:

It is within the Plans of God to destine everyone to eternal life who receives Jesus Christ as their Lord and Savior. Sin in the lives of people who refuse to obey the Word of God is what separates them unto an eternal damnation. Sheol (Hell) has enlarged herself. **(Isaiah 5:14)** It is not God's will that any should perish, but that all men should come to repentance. **(2 Peter 3:9)**

Lesson 26:

Atonement

The Biblical doctrine that God has reconciled sinners to Himself through the sacrificial work of Jesus Christ is called, "Atonement". The doctrine of Atonement spans both Testaments, everywhere pointing to the death, burial and resurrection of Jesus Christ for the sins of the world. We must always keep uppermost in our mind that Jesus Christ is the one who brings together God and man, with salvation as the result of the union. The bible clearly states that Jesus the Christ was the propitiation (price/sacrifice) required by God. **(I John 2:2)**

I. All are invited to find refuge in the atonement of Christ. **(St. Luke 14:16-17)**

II. The apostles plead with sinners to trust in the atoning work of Jesus. **(Acts 2:40; II Cor. 5:20)**

III. All human beings are not only invited, but commanded to believe the gospel.**(Acts 17: 30-31)**

V. Those people who are not "in Christ" will bear the eternal penalty for their own sins. **(Romans 6:23; II Cor. 5:10)**

Summary:

What Jesus accomplished at Calvary extends a personal invitation to everyone born into this world to take advantage of God's atoning plan. Everyone has a right to choose, but they do not have the choice to not choose; because not choosing is a choice in itself.

Lesson 27:

Always Faithful to God!!!

Scripture Text:
II Thess. 3:1-5

Throughout the history of man we find man in a relationship. Even though we see a breach on man's part at certain points in history, we also see God extending His hand, welcoming man back to his Creator. There were those who were faithful to God and there were those who strayed far from the will of God. We are urged to always remain faithful to God, because in Him we live and hope:

I. God is always faithful to us. **(I Cor.1:9; Rev.3:14)**

II. Faithfulness gives us constant access to the throne of God. **(Hebrews 2:17)**

III. Faithfulness displays what's in your heart. **(I Peter 4:19)**

IV. Faithfulness is our reasonable service. **(Tim.3:8; Heb. 12:1-2)**

V. Faithfulness eliminates potential temptations and trials from dominating you. **(I Cor.10:13; Rev. 2:10)**

VI. Faithfulness heightens our awareness to God's call. **(Ephesians 1:1-4; Colossians 1:2-4)**

VII. Faithfulness deepens our commitment to the work at hand. **(I Peter 5:6-11)**

Summary:

God is always faithful to us therefore we should always be faithful to Him.

It is of the Lord's mercies that we are not consumed, because His compassions fail not. They are new every morning: great is thy faithfulness. **(Lamentations 3:22-23)**

Lesson 28:

Are You A Salty Saint or Salt-less Saint?

Scripture Text:
St. Matthews 5:13; Lev. 2:13

Jesus explicitly proclaimed that true Christians are the salt of the earth. When we study the many values of salt we can understand the metaphor being used. Christ made clear to us the importance and significance of sharing the gospel salt. It is through the gospel (good news) that men discover the necessity of a savior and how lost they are from God.

We are spiritual "Salt Shakers" spreading the soul winning salt of Jesus Christ our Lord. Any Christian not willing to obey this Commission is deemed a "Salt-less Saint" and is not fit for the Kingdom of God. Mankind aches for the "gospel salt," it is our job to share it! **(St. Matt. 28:18-20; St. Mark 16:14-18; St. Luke 24:45-49)**

I. Salt brings life and flavor to what it touches.

II. Salt preservcs and decontaminates.

III. Salt purges wounds, enhancing the healing process.

IV. Salt melts the coldness and stiffness of icy conditions.

V. Salt tenderizes toughness.

Summary:

Many of us are living flavorless lives. We've lost our saltiness. In Jesus' day, workmen and soldiers would sometimes be paid with salt. The expression, "not worth his salt" comes from that custom. The word "salary" also derived from the word "salt".

Lesson 29:

Are You Allowing Your Light to Shine?

Scripture Text:
St. Matthew 5:14-16; Isaiah 42:6; 49:6; 60:3

In the study of the "Sermon on the Mount", Jesus not only used salt as a metaphor, but He also used light. It should be understood that salt is what's in you, while light is what others should see coming out of you. As long as you have the "Light" (which is generated by the Holy Ghost and by the power of God's Word) people will see a difference in you. They will see a difference that clearly identifies you as a true Christian and a true child of God. Light is an important ingredient in the character of anyone that is on a mission to win souls for the Kingdom of God.

I. Your Light chases away darkness (sin).

II. Your Light reveals both what's on the inside and outside of you.

III. Your Light is a reflection of who God is and who you are.

IV. Your Light enhances spiritual insight (whether you are the observer or the one being observed).

V. Your Light brightens even more as you grow in relation to God.

Summary:

Light is linked with instruction (Psalms**119:105,130**), truth **(Ps. 43:3**), good **(Isa. 5:20),** salvation **(Ps. 49:6),** life **(Job 33: 28, 30),** peace **(Isa. 45:7),** rejoicing **(Ps. 97:11),** covenant **(Isa. 42:6),** justice and righteousness (**Isa. 59:9**), God's presence and favor **(Ps. 89:15)**

Lesson 30:

Blind Eyes and Deaf Ears

Scripture Text:
Isaiah 29:18; 42:6-9; St. Luke 4:18

It has been long believed that when the Scriptures speak of blind eyes; it's referring only to someone who is visually impaired, physically. Another misconception is when the Scriptures speak of deaf ears; it's speaking only of someone that's unable to hear by natural means.

Blind eyes in certain text denote ignorance as to spiritual things God wants us to see. Deaf ears in certain text denote the inability to hear the spiritual things God is saying to us. With this thought in mind we are wise to ask God to open our spiritual eyes that we may see and open our spiritual ears that we may hear.

I. Many Christians are not aware of the inner ability to see spiritually. (**St. Matthew 15:14; Ephesians 4:17-18**)

II. Many Christians are not aware of the inner ability to hear spiritually. (**Micah 7:16)**

III. We need spiritual eye checkups to make sure we're seeing correctly. (**Isaiah 6:10)**

IV. We need spiritual ear checkups to make sure we're hearing correctly. (**Exodus 4:11; Isaiah 35:5)**

V. We run a risk of missing a more intimate relationship with God and the risk of misunderstanding the written and preached Word of God. (**Isaiah 43:8-11)**

Summary:

Don't neglect your awesome opportunity to see life through the eyes of God. Don't allow the experience of hearing a word from God pass you up because you were not spiritually astute. Your awakening of spiritual senses will be the catalyst through which God will greatly bless you in this life and in the life to come. (**Isaiah 42:5-9)**

Lesson 31:

Blessed or Cursed, It's Your Choice!

Scripture Text:
I Chron. 4:10; Numbers 23:20; Isa. 61:9

To "bless" meant to fill with benefits, either as an end in itself or to make the object blessed a source of further blessing for others. God is most often understood as the agent of blessing in this sense. The concept of cursing was clearly more prevalent in the Old Testament. Depending on who is speaking, one who "curses" is either predicting, praying for, or causing great trouble on someone. Since belonging to God and His people meant blessing, being cursed often meant separation from God and the community of faith.

I. Blessed people bless God with honor and good words (we praise Him). (**Ex. 18:10; Ruth 4:14; Psalms 68:19; Psalms 103:1)**

II. God always bless those who acknowledge His sovereignty.
(Psalms 109:28)

III. Because of "sin" many are under divine condemnation (cursed). **(John 7:49; Gal. 3:10, 13; I Cor. 16:22)**

IV. Many are cursed with a curse by their own doing (disobedience). **(Malachi 3:8-12; Gal. 1:8-9; II Peter 2:14-15; Rev. 16:9, 11, 21)**

V. God bless those who bless His people and curse those who curse them. (**Genesis 12:3; Psalms 33:12**

Summary:

God loves man so much that He gives man the freedom to choose. We have the freedom to choose, but we don't have the freedom to choose the consequences of our choice. Choose to be blessed.

Lesson 32:

Christian Living in a Non-Christian Society

Scripture Text:
Psalms 101:6-8

We live in a society that is constantly changing. The saying, "out with the old and in with the new", has dominated the mind of people of today. Some things are best left as they are and others must be fine-tuned to adapt to the modernizations of time. Regardless of the inconsistencies of people and their needs; God has designed man with an intuition to seek a power greater than himself. Individuals that have chosen to maintain a godly lifestyle based on the teachings of Jesus Christ; are by my definition, true Christians living in a non-Christian society. God demands one thing and society votes for something else. It is societal hunger for change, accompanied by mediocre Christian living that has corrupted the very fiber of home and church cohesion. Below are a few requirements to upholding the standards of true Christian living.

I. Don't compromise with ungodly lifestyles.

II. Stay Prayerful.

III. Fast with consistency.

IV. Study the Word of God.

V. Share the Gospel News with others (both Christian and non-Christian).

VI. Stay busy doing Kingdom Building work (outside and inside church)

VII. Exercise abstinence in regards to questionable behavior.

VIII. Learn to recognize the voice of God (this entails discernment).

IX. Have an unbiased display of true brotherly love.

Summary:

There are three types of Christians:

1) Those who make things happen.
2) Those who watch things happen.
3) Those who ask, "What happened ?"

Lesson 33:

Staying Saved and Sanctified !!!

Scripture Text:
I Thess. 5:23; Eph.2:5

Once upon a time in the life of some; being saved and sanctified meant so much more. As time marched on the dedication and sense of urgency dwindled down to nothing more than just a distant hope. In other words, the hope of glory that use to stir up joy; is now only a passing thought. We must remember, staying saved and sanctified is far more than just religious acts and occasional good deeds. It is a daily order of careful and prayerful living. The Word of God encourages us to be mindful of these things. **(Acts 20:19-21)**

I. Make God a difference between holy and unholy. **(Ezek. 22:26; 44:28)**

II. Set yourself apart from carnal things. **(Lev. 20:7; Joshua 3:5)**

III. Watch for the Lord's return. **(I Thess. 4:13-18; Mk.13:33; Lk.21:36)**

IV. Don't forsake Christian fellowship. **(Heb. 10:24-25)**

V. Love, love, love! **(Rm. 12:10; I Thess. 4:9; Heb. 13:1; Matt. 22:36-40)**

VI. Have an answer concerning your faith. **(John 1:22; I Peter 3:15)**

VII. Have a vision. **(Proverbs 29:18)**

VIII. Put your hands to work. **(Neh. 2:18; 4:17; Gal. 6:9)**

IX. Make an effort to fulfill the Great Commission. **(Matt. 28:18-20)**

X. Never give up on God. **(St. Matt. 6:33; Phil. 1:21)**

XI. Fast as you are led of God. **(Matt. 4:1-2; Acts 14:23; Acts 27:33)**

XII. Pray unceasingly. **(I Thess. 4:17;Luke 18:1; 21:36)**

XIII. Support the church with tithes & offerings **(Mal. 3:8-12; II Cor. 9:7, Luke 6:38)**

Summary:

Blessed is the man that walketh not in the counsel of the ungodly, nor standeth in the way of sinners, nor sitteth in the seat of the scornful. But his delight is in the law of the Lord; and in His law doth he meditate day and night. **(Psalms 1:1-2)**

Lesson 34:

How Pure is Your Religion?

Scripture Text:
James 1:27; Matt. 7:21

The writer of the book of James sets before us the various fruits and manifestations of a genuine relationship with God. James, the preacher of practical righteousness, urges people to prove their faith by a life of benevolent works. He boldly declares that the faith that does not produce works is dead. Faith, by its very nature, cannot exist and be fruitless. It is possible for one to consider himself to have a genuine faith and be mistaken **(Matt. 7:21)**

I. Pure religion has its origin in the heart of God.

II. Pure religion requires that we be teachable in both mind and heart.

III. Pure religion will put forth an earnest effort to control the use of the tongue.

IV. Pure religion involves a constant crusade to eliminate all evil from our hearts and lives.

V. Pure religion reveals itself in the practice of compassionate acts of kindness.

Summary:

As followers of Christ, it is possible for us to have pure religion. To do so we must bring our lives regularly under the searching, penetrating light of the life and teachings of our Lord.

Pure religion will produce joy in our own hearts. Pure religion is contagious. Many of the unsaved about us will become attracted to our Savior if they can see a living demonstration of what it means to be a Christian in our daily conduct.

Lesson 35:

The Blessed Gift of Sleep

Scripture Text:
Various

One of the beautiful revelations of Scripture is that sleep is a gift of God for those He loves. David found himself under tremendous pressures surrounded by enemies on every side, his very life threatened. Yet in the midst of it all he knows the blessedness of untroubled, restful sleep.

There are many today who do not have this blessed assurance. They wake with fear and with the torment of sleeplessness. The worries and cares of the day follow them into the night. There is a blessing in knowing your soul is safe in the Lord's keeping. You can sleep peacefully and awake without fear and anxiety.

I. The Lord sustains you. **(Psalms 3:5; Jude 24)**

II. The Lord makes you dwell in safety. **(Psalms 4:8; 91:1)**

III. The Lord enables you to mentally lie down in peace. **(Psalms 23:2; Isaiah 26:3)**

IV. The Lord will minister to you throughout your rest. **(Psalms 130 :6)**

V. The Lord promised rest to His people. **(Psalms 127:2; Matt. 11:28-29)**

VI. The Lord has a watchful eye on His children. **(I Peter 3:12)**

VII. The Lord summons you to cast your cares upon Him. **(I Peter 5:7)**

Summary:

Can't sleep? If counting sheep doesn't work, try talking to the Shepherd. Believe God and know that He loves you and want you to experience daily the blessed gift of sleep.

Suggested Prayer:

I disown and rebuke the spirit of insomnia in my life. I also release into my life peace and the blessed gift of sleep. This I pray In Jesus Name . Amen

Lesson 36:

Obeying God-The Currency for Heaven's Blessings!

Scripture Text:
Various

We are continually presented with choices in our families, jobs, finances, and even in our relationships with God our Father. The question we must ask ourselves if we want to be blessed of the Father is: Where does the Lord fit in the decisions we make? The truth is, we will never go wrong as long as we obey God. We see this principle confirmed time after time throughout the pages of Scripture. Obey God and leave all the consequences to Him. This is always the right course of action. How can we be sure to stay on track?

I. Recognize that your willingness to submit to the Lord depends on what you believe about Him. **(James 4:7; II Samuel 22:45; Psalms 18:44)**

II. Continue to trust the Father, regardless of your circumstances.
(Proverbs 3:5-6; Psalms 4:5)

III. Grow in your love toward the Father.
(Mark 12:30; John 15:9)

IV. Don't just talk to God, but also listen to Him.
(Isaiah 55:3; Jeremiah 13:15)

V. Realize obeying the Lord will require courage and full surrender. **(Exodus 19:5; Deuteronomy 30:2; I Peter 4:17)**

Summary:

Believe in God's sovereignty. Increase in your trust for Him. Grow deeper in your intimate relationship with Him. Listen to Him intently. Surrender yourself to Him fully and courageously.

Lesson 37:

The Things that Really Count!!!

Scripture Text:
Philippians 3:1-9

The apostle Paul took pride in his rituals, relationships, respectability, race, religion, and reputation and he discovered that in spite of his religion and legalism, he was bankrupt, blind and bound for hell.

The things that Paul counted as loss were not bad in and of themselves, they were mostly good. A good thing is a bad thing if it keeps you from the best thing.

When Paul ceased from relying upon himself for salvation and turned to Jesus Christ, he found three things: a knowledge of Christ, a fellowship with Christ, and the righteousness of Christ.

I. A Knowledge of Christ:

Paul considered the knowledge of Christ to surpass anything he could ever attain on his own. This isn't knowledge as in gaining information. Here Paul used it to describe spiritual intimacy between himself and God. Knowledge is more than what we think inside our heads, it is what we experience in our heart in a personal relationship with our Lord Jesus Christ.

II. A Fellowship with Christ:

Paul said that he wanted to "be found in Him." Before Paul's conversion, he had religion. After his salvation, Paul had a relationship, the most important being the one he had with his Savior the Lord Jesus Christ.

III. **A Righteousness of Christ:**

The closer Paul drew to God, the greater his awareness of his own filthiness and need of the righteousness of Christ. Without the imputation of Christ's righteousness into our lives, we would have no relationship whatsoever with God. Our righteousness does not come by works. It is an imputed righteousness **(Romans 4:21-25).** This means that the righteousness of Christ was put on our account by our Lord and Savior Jesus Christ. He paid for it on Calvary's cross.

Summary:

When God looks at the ledger of our lives, He sees red not in a bad way, but a good way. He sees the red, righteous, royal blood of His Son credited to our account and we are declared righteous before Him. These are the things that really count

Lesson 38:

The Timeless Authority of God's Word

One of the unique characteristics of God's Word is the awesome quality of not being restricted to time. Time will never out live the resounding truth or authoritative Words that come forth from the mouth of God.

I. The Word of God is unique.
(St. Matt. 4:4; St. Matt.8:16; Heb. 4:12)

II. The Word of God is not restricted to time.
(Ps. 33:9; St. John 1:1-2; St. Matt. 5:18 ; St. John 6:68; Rev. 14:6-7)

III. The Word of God produces a godly life, if obeyed.
(Ps. 33:6 ; Rom. 10:17 ; II Tim. 3:16 ; St. John 5:37-40 Ps. 119:11; Ps. 119:105-106)

IV. The Word of God addresses your issues in life.
(Ps. 68:20; St. John 17:17-19 ; Isaiah 40:6-8)

Summary:

Every Christian should have an answer concerning his or her faith. Their established faith should rest on the resounding truth and timeless authority of the Word of God.

Lesson 39:

The Real Truth about Christmas is Christ!

If you're not aware of the truth about Christmas you're probably feeling a sense of urgency and chaos; which in turn produces stress and frustration. Christmas was never meant to be that way. Commercialism and unbiblical views has clouded the real meaning behind this blessed event. The spirit of Christmas has been tainted and misconstrued by untrue ideologies. God is pointing us back to scripture for our rediscovery of the truth about Christmas. The real truth about Christmas is Christ.

I. Christmas is not about what you want; it's about who you need. (You need a savior, **St. Luke 2:10-11; St. Matt. 1:18-25)**

II. The Christmas truth has been clouded by the spirit of commercialism. Black Friday, Small Business Saturday, Cyber Monday **(Prov. 23:5; Matt.6:31-34; Matt.13:22)**

III. Stress and frustration at Christmas are results of an untrue perspective. **(St. Matt. 22:29; Heb. 12:1-3; I Tim. 6:6)**

IV. The spirit of Christmas produces a solemn peace. **(St. Luke 2:14; Romans 5:1b; I Tim. 6:7)**

V. Truth is a universal commodity.

VI. Keep Christ in the mass. (No X-mas)

VII. We honor the birth of our Savior in His coming to this sinful world to save us. **(St. Luke 2:11)**

Summary:

Discover the truth about Christmas by returning to the biblical account where the first announcement and celebration of Christmas took place. Invite Christ back into your Christmas this year and receive the gift that keeps on giving.

Lesson 40:

A Spiritual Self-Examination

(answer questions below)

1. Have I repented of my sins? Yes or No

2. Am I Saved? Yes or No

3. Am I baptized in Jesus' name? Yes or No

4. Do I believe in the gift of the Holy Ghost? Yes or No

5. Have I spoken in tongues as mentioned in Acts 2:4, as evidence of God's indwelling Spirit? Yes or No

6. Do I fast as an individual? Yes or No

7. Do I fast corporately? (with the church) Yes or No

8. Do I pray as an individual? Yes or No

9. Do I pray corporately? (at church) Yes or No

10. Do I study the Bible? Yes or No

11. Am I a backslider? Yes or No

12. Where do I want to spend eternity? Heaven or Hell

13. Do I steal, cheat, fornicate, or adulterate? Yes or No

14. Am I a gossiper or liar? Yes or No

15. Do I smoke? Yes or No

16. Do I drink alcoholic beverages? Yes or No

17. Do I take drugs (of any kind) to get high? Yes or No

18. Am I single? Happy or Sad (be honest with yourself)

19. Am I married? Happy or Sad (ditto)

20. Am I selfish, materialistic or money hungry? Yes/ No

21. Am I self-righteous? Yes or No

Summary:

Life is a coin. You can spend it any way you wish, but you can only spend it once.

Scripture Reference: **(James 4:14)** (your life is but a vapor)

Lesson 41:

"Blessed Prosperity"

Scripture Text:
Psalm 1;119:33-34

"Blessed"; the opening word of the Psalms contains the essence of all that is to follow. The blessings they unfold flow into two directions: from God to man, and from man back again to God. David goes on to sum up the blessedness promised to man in one brief, expressive sentence: "Whatever he does prosper." How can you be such a person – blessed of God so that whatever you do prospers? David lays down five conditions:

I. **You must not walk in the counsel of the un-godly (wicked).**
(The counsel you follow determines the course of your life).

II. **You must not stand in the way of sinners.**
(This is a metaphor used to discourage sinful ways/behavior).

III. **You must not sit in the seat of the scornful (mockers).**
(Don't find comfort in talking bad about other people).

IV. **You must delight in the law of the Lord.**
(Find pleasure in God's statutes, even when they expose you).

V. **You must meditate on it (God's Law) day and night.**
(The ultimate source of all wise and righteous counsel is the law of the Lord. If you fill your heart and mind continually with His law, and if you direct your life according to it, then blessing and prosperity are your God–appointed portion).

Summary:

Perhaps you are weary of frustration and failure. Take heed to these rules. Meditate on them. Apply them. They will work in your life. God Himself guarantees you success.

Lesson 42:

Trusting God beyond Comprehension

Scripture Text:
Isaiah 55:7-9

The assumption that you will comprehend how God will answer certain prayers is one of the leading causes of faith failure. There is no guarantee that God will always answer your prayers exactly the same way. He is not restricted to any boundaries of any kind. He is not subject to limitations of any kind. He is sovereign in every aspect. The inability on man's part to under-stand the what, when, where, why and how of God has been a major roadblock and hindrance to the necessary flow of faith. Unwavering faith is a must. It is a display of trust that moves God to respond to our petitions. **(Heb. 10:23; Jas. 1:6)**

We must not allow our intellect to get in the way of our faith. If you choose to see where you're stepping or if you're afraid to step before you move, it's no longer faith.

I. Trusting God requires walking by faith and not by sight. **(II Cor. 5:7-9)**

II. Faith in itself is the substratum: there can be no substitute**. (Heb. 11:6)**

III. We mustn't lean to our own intellect. **(Proverbs 3:3-5)**

IV. In trusting God we should be in preparation for manifestation**. (2 Kings 4:1-7)**

V. Faith walking in many cases is incomprehensible to us**. (Hebrews 11:30)**

VI. Challenges by unbelieving intellects sometimes occur**. (St. Matt. 22:15, 23, 35)**

Summary:

"Testing God" is not the same as "Trusting God". In **testing** God the person believes in the end only if they achieve in the end. In **trusting** God the person achieves in the end because they believed to the end.

Lesson 43:

The Privilege of Prayer

Scripture Reference:
I Thess. 5:17

We are privileged by Our Heavenly Father to communicate with Him at any given time. That time we communicate with Him is defined as a "time of prayer". Such a privilege is granted to us because of the love of God shown to us even before we were born into this world. God had a plan and we are the beneficiaries of that plan.

As a result of Jesus dying for the sins of the world mankind is privileged to boldly approach the throne of Grace. **(Hebrews 4:16**) The only requirement by God is that we believe on His only begotten Son as our Lord and Savior. (**St. John 1:12; 3:16)**

Many professing Christians unwittingly neglect the ever-present opportunity to converse with God the Father. My utmost desire and prayer is that we all come into the knowledge of exercising the "Privilege of Prayer" to its' fullest capacity.

I. Don't just ask something of God. Learn to worship and to thank Him.

II. God awaits a steady communication with us.

III. God is never too busy to converse with His children.

IV. No one's prayer is insignificant.

V. The privilege to pray is not a time to complain to God.

VI. Enjoy the ever present help of God.

VII. Make praying to the Father your first fruit of the day.

VIII. Pray silently (within your soul)

IX. Pray audibly (out loud)

X. End your day with prayer before going to bed.

Summary:

Not all Christians enjoy the privilege of prayer. Some assume their schedule doesn't allow them time to pray. This is a mistake and a trick of the flesh to rob the Christian of the joyous experience of truly knowing the Father. The real truth is that no one professing a life of Christianity can afford to not have a life dedicated to constant communication with God.

Lesson 44:

The King Has Come!

Scripture Text:
St. Matt. 2:1-11

As astonishing as it may be, the King of all was born as a babe in the town of Bethlehem. He was adored and worshiped by all men everywhere. **(Micah 5:2**) "For the Kingdom of God is not meat and drink; but righteousness, and peace, and joy in the Holy Ghost" **(Romans 14:17).**

The King is Born

I. The Search for the King – (**St. Matthew 2:1-4)**

II. The Finding of the King – (**St. Matthew 2:5-11)**

The King Lives

I. His entrance into Jerusalem – (**Zechariah 9:9)**

II. His testimony to Pilate – (**St. John 19:19)**

III. His reign in our hearts – (**Psalms 24:7-8; Philippians 2:8-10)**

Even though Jesus came as a baby, He came already equipped with the ability to perform the task of redeeming man back to God. He came as a baby, yet He was before all things. **(St. John 1:1)** He died as a criminal, yet He lives as the Righteous Judge and King. **(Revelation 16:7)**

Summary:

Jesus, Son of God and King of Kings came and walked every step ordained for Him in Scripture. He never neglected any part of His task assigned by God the Father. He exemplified the truth that in life there are no shortcuts to victory. **(Zechariah 14:9)**

Lesson 45:

The Discipleship of the Twelve!

Scripture Text:
St. Matt. 4:17-23; Luke 6:40

True disciples of the Lord Jesus must believe in Him, deny themselves, accept their place in Christ's kingdom, and be faithful in performing His will and work unto death.

Jesus chose discipleship as His plan to reach the world. Today we must exercise the same passion and commitment displayed by Christ in discipling people into the Kingdom of God. It is essential that we understand our commission as did the twelve disciples.

True Discipleship

I. The Meaning of Discipleship

II. The Development of a Disciple

III. The Continuing Process of Discipling Converts **(St. John 15:16)**

Requirements of Discipleship

I. The Privilege of Being a Disciple

II. The Demands for Being Disciples **(St. Luke 14:25-33)**

III. The Reward of Being a Disciple **(St. Matt. 5:12)**

The Disciple's Relationships

I. Relationship with Christ.

II. Relationship with His Natural Family.

III. Relationship with His Spiritual Family **(St. John 13:34 35)**

The Disciple's Commitment

I. Persecuted for Christ's Name Sake **(St. Matt. 5:10-11; 10:22-25; Romans 8:35-39)**

II. Faithful until Death **(II Timothy 4:6-8)**

Summary:

The twelve disciples were not people chosen from the upper class of citizens of that day. They were ordinary people that were chosen by God to do extraordinary things. We are not limited by our ordinary social status when it comes to our call to do Kingdom work.

Lesson 46:

We Need an Awakening; Let it Rain!

Scripture Text:
Joel 3:9-11; Romans 13:11; Luke 9:32; Ephesians 5:14

The devastating fact is that many of us strong Christians are asleep and don't know it. We have not allowed our mind and heart to be sensitized to the voice of God. We have subconsciously drowned out His sweet and reasoning voice of warnings against complacency.

As a result of our sleeping, the young and inexperienced Christians are being picked off by the devil. It is time to wake with a spirit of urgency and diligence so we can successfully take back those that have become prisoners to the spirit of this present darkness. Yes, the darkness of this wicked society known as the world. In the spirit realm, victims are corralled into a barnyard as though they are mindless cattle. They are draped in dull colored hoodies with a darkened face mask made of mesh. How long will we remain asleep and how many more souls will we allow the enemy to pluck from amongst us. I say, not one more. I say I want them all back and I want them back NOW!

We need an awakening, down pouring buckets of rain upon us to wake us from the deep sleep of complacency that has numbed us far too long. If we are going to be victorious in this fight against the enemy we need to strike now. All hands on deck! We need every one that is named a man or woman of God to take up arms and prepare for battle.

Our mission is to destroy anything that is not like Christ. Our mission is to stain the battlefield with the blood of Satan and all his imps that has strategically manipulated themselves into the fellowship of the saints. We are not ignorant to his wicked devices. We are not powerless to overthrow the strongholds he has placed on the feeble and weak Christians that have fallen prey to his snares.

We must dismantle every set trap. We must annihilate every bunker, every foxhole, every demonic sniper and every foot soldier sent by the enemy to depress, stress and undress the people of God.

Where does this fight take place? Answer: Right here! When does this fight take place? Answer: Right Now!

Lesson 47:

How to Handle the Epidemic of Scandal!!!

Scripture Text:
James 3:2-18; I Peter 3:8-17

The word "scandal" is defined as a disgraceful or discreditable action or circumstance. The result of scandal leads to defamatory (insulting) talk and malicious (evil intent) gossip. The unfortunate thing about scandal in the life of a believer is that it spreads like an epidemic.

It has the effects of a deadly disease. Another disheartening thing is that the scandal is sometimes based on lies. The devil loves this particular attack because of its lasting and lingering ability to continue to defame the life of a believer. The nature of the sinfulness of man is to always have some dirt on another's character, so as to discredit the legitimacy as to who they are. The tongue of man is a deadly poison that has ended the lives and careers of many throughout the ages. **(James 3:8-10)** There are a number of ways to handle scandal but let us take the godly approach:

I. Remember, no one can truly point a finger at another without implying self. **(Psalms 51:5; John 8:7, Romans 3:23)**

II. Don't spend valuable time chasing down scandalous accusations. **(St. Mark 15:3; I Timothy 6:20)**

III. Trust God that your life as a true Christian will overshadow the attacks of the enemy. **(Psalms 27:2; Psalms 56:4; Proverbs 16:7; Isaiah 54:17; Isaiah 59:19;Romans 12:20)**

IV. Pray for God's Divine intervention on your behalf. **(Psalms 55:17; Psalms 145:19; James 5:16b)**

V. Be ready to forgive your trespassers and scandalizers. **(St. Matt. 5:44; 6:12; Luke 17:3)**

VI. Stay busy and preoccupy yourself by doing the Lord's work. **(I Cor. 15:58)**

VII. Abstain from any questionable persons or activities that may lead to further accusations.**(I Thessalonians 5:22)**

Summary:

I would like to briefly suggest to anyone that finds delight in scandalizing others to take caution, you are setting yourself up to reap what you have sown. For most people it is hard to tolerate the very thing they inflict upon others. In my closing, scandal is sinful and it eats away at the very fiber of what God has ordained of His people. **(Proverbs 6:12-19)** Don't allow yourself to become the scandalizing mouthpiece either. As stated in the title of this lesson; scandal is an epidemic, a sickening disease. Scandal is not a new strategy of Satan to destroy someone's life; it's an old strategy of Satan that's only effective if there are willing participants.

Lesson 48:

Five Purposes of God Accomplished Through Suffering

Scripture Text:
II Corinthians 12:7-8; James 1:2-4

The modern day thought is, "Get all you can and can all you get." This line of thinking is detrimental to the growth of anyone serious about their walk with the Lord. If our hope is in things, we run the risk of not exercising hope in God. It is obvious through biblical accounts that God in His wise providence has chosen suffering as a means of displaying our misplacements. Below are five purposes of God accomplished through suffering.

I. God uses suffering to reveal our spiritual character. **(II Chronicles 32:31)**

II. God uses suffering to keep us from exalting ourselves. **(II Corinthians 12:6-7)**

III. God uses suffering to draw us to Himself. **(Philippians 2:13)**

IV. God uses suffering to display His grace. **(Deuteronomy 33:26-29)**

V. God uses suffering to perfect His power. **(II Corinthians 12:9)**

Summary:

Suffering reveals both God and man and where they stand with each other. Remember, God has not promised you smooth sailing, but He has promised you a safe landing.

Lesson 49:

No One Has A Pointless Life!!!

Scripture text:
Psalms 34:1-12; Luke 12:15

Definition: Pointless – without meaning, useless, of no real value.

I. Life is a gift from God. **(Psalms 139:14 – 18)**

II. You must learn to love yourself and grow onward in life.

III. Don't allow past failures in life to dictate your future in life.

IV. God has wonderful plans for your life. **(Jer. 29:11-13)**

Summary:

In contrast to Forrest Gump, life is not like a box of chocolates, because when your steps are ordered by the Lord you can always anticipate in life what you are going to get.

–Pastor Ronnie Whittier

Lesson 50:

The Explanation for our Difficulties

Scripture Text:
John 17:21

If you are going through a time of isolation, seemingly all alone, read (**John 17**). It will explain exactly why you are where you are—because Jesus has prayed that you "may be one" with the Father as He is. Are you helping God to answer that prayer, or do you have some other goal for your life? Since you became a disciple, you cannot be as independent as you used to be.

God reveals in (**John 17**) that His purpose is not just to answer our prayers, but that through prayer we might come to discern His mind. Yet there is one prayer which God must answer, and that is the prayer of Jesus—"… that they may be one just as we are one …" (**17:22**). Are we as close to Jesus Christ as that?

God is not concerned about our plans; He doesn't ask, "Do you want to go through this loss of a loved one, this difficulty, or this defeat?" No, He allows these things for His own purpose.

The things we are going through are either making us sweeter, better, and nobler men and women, or they are making us more critical and fault-finding, and more insistent on our own way. The things that happen either make us evil, or they make us more saintly, depending entirely on our relationship with God and its level of intimacy.

If we will pray, regarding our own lives, "Your will be done" (**Matthew 26:42**), then we will be encouraged and comforted by (**John 17**), knowing that our Father is working according to His own wisdom, accomplishing what is best. When we understand God's purpose, we will not become small-minded and cynical. Jesus prayed nothing less for us than absolute oneness with Himself, just as He was one with the Father. Some of us are far from this oneness;

yet God will not leave us alone until we *are* one with Him—because Jesus prayed, "… that they *all* may be one … ."

Lesson 51:

God's Fail-Proof Financial Plan!!!

(Part 1)

God speaks to us about our finances because He knows that "where your heart is, there you will be also" **(Matt. 6:21)**

I. Identify your financial problem area for what it is. **(Haggai 1:1-9; Mal. 3:9)**

II. Get in line with the Word of God regarding your tithes and offerings. **(Gen. 28:22b; Lev. 27:30; Matt. 23:23)**

III. God has an unfailing plan for blessing our finances and it is discovered through our obedience to His Word. **(Deut. 8:3; I Sam. 15:22 – 23a; Mal. 3:7-8; Matt. 4:4)**

IV. Trust God's plan for your financial breakthrough. (**Prov. 3:9-10; Mark 6:38; II Cor. 9:7)**

Summary:

Of the 38 recorded parables told by Jesus Christ, 16 deal with man's use of finances: how he secures his money, saves his money, spends his money, or shares his money. As a matter of fact, one out of every ten verses in the Gospels deals with personal finances.

Lesson 52:

God's Fail-Proof Financial Plan

(Part 2)

God has the final word on everything, including your finances. The Bible contains principles for financial security which, if followed, will lead to long-term financial independence for you and your family. The thread of generosity is woven completely and inextricably into the very fabric of Christ's teachings. Jesus offered this guiding principle: "Freely you have received, freely give" **(Matthew 10:8)**

I. It's quite simple; when you give, you receive. **(Luke 6:38; Acts 20:35)**

II. Give with cheerful and godly contentment. **(II Cor. 9:7; I Timothy 6:6-10)**

III. Don't miss the opportunity to bless God in your giving. **(II Samuel 24:18-25)**

IV. Freely giving offers a spirit of freedom from financial bondage. **(Acts 2:42-47)**

Summary:

Your best plan is only a plan without the blessings of God upon it. Apply God's fail-proof financial plan of tithes and offerings to your budget and experience the blessing of God's guidance to financial freedom.

Lesson 53:

Identifying And Breaking Generational Curses

Many Christians battle within themselves to break free of the ancestral stereotype of generational curses or strongholds. Their families are bound by repetitive encounters with spirits of drunkenness, violent deaths, sexual promiscuity and other spirits assigned to them by Satan.

The devices of the enemy are so manipulative that a person may assume that God Himself has placed a generational curse upon their family. Once you begin to believe such a lie, Satan is well on his way to controlling your ancestral thought life. You must identify the root of the stronghold or curse Satan has assigned to your family and reverse the curse. You must not allow his wicked devices to manipulate your family anymore. Satan may have entered your life through a door opened by your ancestors, but God has equipped you through the power of the Holy Ghost to close that door forever. **(St. John 8:36; Ezekiel 18:20)**

I. First things first – **REPENT** – Accept the salvation God is offering through the shed blood of His only begotten son – **JESUS CHRIST. (St. John 3:3-7; 14-17)**

II. Encourage your family members both young and old to seek God immediately. **(Joshua 24:15 ; 2 Cor.6:2)**

III. We were all under curses before we got saved, but in Jesus, old things are passed away . **(2 Cor.5:17 ; St. John 7:49)**

V. God will preserve and protect your family. **(2 Tim. 4:18; Jude 24-25)**

Summary:

Where Jesus is there is liberty, He welcomes your family to join His family**. (2 Cor. 3:17; Romans 8:14-16; Rev. 22:3)**

Lesson 54:

Continued Consecration Is A Must!!!

Scripture Ref.
Exodus 13:2, 12, 15; Num. 3:12

Consecration is defined as the act of devoting or setting yourself apart for worship or service to God. It is not a one-time experience but an ongoing process. Continue in separating yourself from things that can be detrimental to your salvation. Be steadfast in looking to God everyday of your life. Below are a few pointers on staying consecrated throughout the year.

I. Consecration is a choice you must make. **(I Chronicles 29:2-9)**

II. Consecration is a vital ingredient to your spiritual growth.**(Exodus 32:29)**

III. Consecration can be a lonely road. **(Leviticus 8:33-35)**

IV. Consecration begins but should never end. **(Exodus 29:9)**

V. Consecration is not stagnated by trials and tribulations. (**Micah 4:13**)

Summary:

Consecration must not be a seasonal event that only occurs when an individual deems it necessary. It would be wise of the dedicated Christian to make this requirement an everyday occurrence throughout the year.

Lesson 55:

Is Your Mind Stayed on God?

Scripture Text:
Isaiah 26:3

Is your mind stayed on God or is it starved? Starvation of the mind, caused by neglect, is one of the chief sources of exhaustion and weakness in a servant's life. If you have never used your mind to place yourself before God, begin to do it now. There is no reason to wait for God to come to you. You must turn your thoughts and your eyes away from the face of idols and look to Him and be saved (see **Isaiah 45:22**).

Your mind is the greatest gift God has given you and it ought to be devoted entirely to Him. You should seek to be "bringing every thought into captivity to the obedience of Christ …"
(**2 Corinthians 10:5**). This will be one of the greatest assets of your faith when a time of trial comes, because then your faith and the Spirit of God will work together. When you have thoughts and ideas that are worthy of credit to God learn to compare and associate them with all that happens in nature—the rising and the setting of the sun, the shining of the moon and the stars, and the changing of the seasons. You will begin to see that your thoughts are from God as well and your mind will no longer be at the mercy of your impulsive thinking, but will always be used in service to God.

Summary:

Remember whose you are and whom you serve. Encourage yourself to remember, and your affection for God will increase tenfold. Your mind will no longer be starved, but will be quick and enthusiastic, and your hope will be inexpressibly bright.

Lesson 56:

True Repentance and True Sorrow

True repentance and true sorrow should work together. To separate one from the other is to raise a question of sincerity. Unfortunately, many make the assumption that repentance and sorrow are only outward gestures. True repentance and true sorrow are generated from the depth of one's heart.

I. Sorrow and desire for forgiveness are aspects of repentance. **(Psalms 51:1; II Cor.7:9)**

II. True sorrow produces sincere repentance without regret. **(Matt. 21:32; Psalms 38:18)**

III. Repentance is sanctioned by God. **(II Tim.2:25; Acts 5:31; Acts 11:18)**

V. Godly sorrow work repentance to salvation. **(II Cor. 7:8 -11)**

Summary:

Sorrow leading to repentance is essentially a change of mind and a change of heart. The intricate weaving of these two ingredients has the potential to change the trajectory of one's entire life.

Lesson 57:

Unity – (The Power of One)

Throughout the ages there have been many stories of victorious things done at the hands of only a few. Within our history books we read of miraculous accomplishments done by groups of least likely candidates. We still marvel today of great feats that occurred long before many of us were ever born.

As we examine the pages of time we find within these stories a common ingredient. We see a similar and familiar action known as Unity. This single thread of power enables people to reach goals they never thought were possible.

Unity is a quality of character we also find heavily sprinkled throughout the stories of the Bible. Many of the patriarchs and matriarchs of scripture possessed the God- given ability to encourage people to work together. Such great leaders as Noah, Moses, Joshua, Esther, Deborah , Gideon, Nehemiah and Peter just to name a few. These men and women of God understood that God works through people, especially people that are Kingdom Builders. People that have a common cause, that cause being so well defined that it seems to be the voice of one.

Inscribed on the currency used in the United States of America is written the phrase " E Pluribus Unum" which means, "Out of Many Comes One". Written above many institutions of higher learning we see the word "University" which derived from two words, Unity and Diversity. When we put Unity with anything we endeavor to do to the Glory of God, those immortal words, "The Power of One" is quickly activated in our lives.

More Servings of Manna

Blessed are they that do hunger and thirst after righteousness for they shall be filled.
St. Matthew 5:6

Lesson 1:

Tearing down or Building up?

The Bible tells us that just like a building is built up, we must build up the body of Christ through how we function with one another, how we treat one another, and how we encourage one another. According to **(I Cor.3:9)**, we are God's building. We build it up externally through evangelism. We build it up internally by strengthening, encouraging, and ministering to the members of the body so they can have the strength to go on and serve God in a world that is hostile to everything we believe. Here are a few suggestions for the builders of the body of Christ:

I. Edification is not about yourself; it's about the saints. **(I Cor. 10:23-24;Ephesians 4:11-12; Romans 14:19)**

II. It's not what you profess, it's what you pursue. **(Matt. 6:33)**

III. It's not about how much you know; it's about how much you care. **(I Cor. 8:1)**

IV. It's not about your gifts; it's about your goals. **(I Cor. 12:31-13:1; Philippians 1:27; I Cor. 9:25)**

V. It's not your wisdom; it's about His Word. **(Heb. 4:12; Psalms 119:11; Psalms 119:105)**

Summary:

Ask God first of all to build you up through His Word so you can then have a ministry in helping to build up others.

Lesson 2:

How to Protect Your Faith

While great opportunity awaits, so does great temptation and confusion. In fact, the apostle Paul spoke to his young student and friend, Timothy, about this very issue. "Some have rejected these and so have shipwrecked their faith" **(I Tim. 1:18-19).** There are a number of ways to avoid this pitfall. Below are a few suggestions on how you can protect your faith.

I. Make a commitment to Community. **(Heb. 10:23)**

Walk with, pray with, encourage, be around and be accountable to other people who share your faith.

II. Make a commitment to Service. **(James 2:14)**

Get involved in serving other people, especially those who are marginalized, disenfranchised, those on the fringes of society. The more you get involved in pouring life into others, the less intimidating your struggles and your questions seem.

III. Make a Commitment to Grow. **(I Peter 2:1-2)**

Read your bible. Study it even if you have questions, even if you have doubts, even if you have struggles. Continue growing in the Word and in your faith.

Summary:

Use your faith or lose your faith. It <u>will</u> work if you work it.

<u>Lesson 3:</u>

Thank God for Pressure

Scripture Text:
II Corinthians 1:1-11

Today's world is full of pressure. Paul wrote II Corinthians in response to the pressures he faced. Yet, while he detailed his stress points in **II Corinthians**, he also sounded a note of triumph. The first word in the body of the book is praise.

I. Pressure leads to God's Comfort. **(vv.3-4)**

II. Pressure equips us to comfort others. **(vv.4-5)**

III. Pressure produces patient endurance. **(v.6)**

IV. Pressure teaches us to rely on God. **(vv. 8-9)**

V. Pressure generates Prayer and Thanksgiving. **(vv.10-11)**

Summary:

What pressures have been weighing on you lately? I challenge you to make them into a prayer list, take them home, and spend some time before the Lord in praise and trust Him with the results.

Lesson 4:

The Extraordinary Christian

Scripture Text:
Psalms 1:1-3; 37:4

Sometimes the greatest enemy of the world isn't the worst things we do in life; it can also be the good. We become content with the ordinary good we do and we are not aspired to do anymore. Don't be content to be an ordinary Christian. Make an effort to be an extraordinary Christian and you will be a happy Christian. Observe a few characteristics of the Extraordinary Christian:

I. The Extraordinary Christian is separated from the world. **(v.1)**

Like our Lord, we should be different but not distant; consistent, not discouraged. You'll never move the world if you're moved by the world. **(II Cor. 4:8-11)**

II. The Extraordinary Christian is saturated in the Law of the Lord. **(v.2)**

In what is your delight, the Word or the world? **(Ps. 37:4)**

III. The Extraordinary Christian sends forth his fruit in season **(v.3).**

What is the fruit of the Christian? New Christians! When is the last time you have shared the gospel, or even thought about the salvation of others? **(Matt. 7:16-17; Jn. 4:36; Gal. 5:22; Col. 1:9-10)**

Summary:

Being extraordinary is actually quite simple: be separate from the world, saturated in the Word, and boldly spreading the gospel of Christ.

Lesson 5:

It's a Matter of the Heart

Scripture Text:
St. Mark 4:1-20

Definition: Heart- the whole personality; the emotional or moral as distinguished from the intellectual nature; the innermost being.

Introduction:

There is an old saying, "Crime doesn't pay… and neither does farming." Jesus' parable about sowing, growing, and harvesting, made perfect sense to His audience. In this story about a farmer sowing seed, Jesus mentions four types of dirt. He then turns to explain what each means:

I. Hard Dirt **(v.2):** The Hard Heart **(v. 14-15)**

II. Rocky Dirt **(v. 5-6):** The Shallow Heart **(v. 16-17)**

III. Thorny Dirt **(v.7):** The Overcrowded Heart **(v. 18-19)**

IV. Good Dirt **(v. 8):** The Good Heart **(v. 20)**

Summary:

In what condition is your heart? How can you know? You can know by taking a spiritual EKG.

E- Examine your heart
K- Know for sure your heart belongs to Jesus
G- Grow

Lesson 6:

Getting it Right When you have done it All Wrong

Scripture Text:
Psalm 51

Introduction:

We all struggle with this thing called sin (doing what we know we shouldn't and failing to do what we know we should). We can learn from scripture how to deal with our sin. David, in (**Psalm 51**) shows us how to do what the Bible calls repentance:

I. Face the Facts. **(v. 1-5)**

II. Ask God to change you from the Inside Out. **(v. 6-12)**

III. Accept God's Forgiveness. **(v. 13-19)**

Summary:

Is there anything in your life you haven't faced up to yet? Are you running from your sin or trying to change yourself? Follow the example given here in Scripture and experience the restoration God has provided through our Lord and Savior Jesus Christ.

Lesson 7:

Six Faith Strengthening Principles

Scripture Text:
Hebrews 11:8-13

One of the biggest problems a Christian encounters is when his faith seems to have lost its effectiveness. That odd feeling of bewilderment can be quite misleading sometimes. It tends to make the believer second guess everything pertaining to his belief. This as we know is evident of the handy work of the enemy Satan. When your faith is under attack return to the roots of your faith and be reassured that the Holy Spirit is yet operating in spite of your feelings.

Here are six principles when put into action that will reassure your faith:

I. The Voice Principle: We must hear from God. (**Hebrews 11:8; Romans 10:17**)

   A. Faith does not come from guessing at the will of God. **(I John 5:14; Heb.1:1-3)**

II. The Venture Principle**:** We must obey what we know. **(Hebrews 11:8)**

   A. Our responsibility is not to totally understand, but to readily obey.

   B. If you're having a faith problem, you're probably having an obedience problem.

III. The Value Principle: We must establish Priorities. **(Hebrews 11:9-10)**

A. Our citizenship is in Heaven. **(Philippians 3:20)**

B. We must not act like or be conformed to the world. **(I John 2:15-17; Rom. 12:2)**

IV. The Vision Principle: We must keep our faith focused. **(Hebrews 11:10; 11:13; Col. 3; 1-2; 11:1; 2 Cor. 4:18)**

A. Faith is setting your affection on something that is bigger than most of us are living for.

V. The Vigilance Principle: We must guard our hearts. **(Heb. 11:11; I Peter 1:7)**

A. Be subject unto God and resist the devil. **(James 4:7)**

VI. The Victory Principle: Enjoy the Blessings. **(Hebrews 11:11-12)**

A. There is no way you can live in victory apart from faith. **(Romans 5:1)**

Summary:

Faith is the mark of a Christian. We have the written Word of God and we have the indwelling of the Holy Spirit; meaning our faith is built on an unshakeable foundation. Rise above your feelings and exercise your God given faith.

Lesson 8:

Your Trials Unveil Your Purpose!

Scripture Text:
Romans 8:28; James 1:2-4; I Peter 4:12

Our character is often tested without warning. We are often at a loss to even find words to describe our situation. Given the inescapable fact that we must not only face trials in this life, we're also tackled by the things that come along with "going through." The disloyalty of family and friends and the absence of love from Fellow-Christians making it seem as though the world is caving in on top of you. Within the confines of our general theme, "The Commanded Blessing" there is at least three things that God is doing in us through trials. These trials unveil our purpose, thus releasing "The Commanded Blessing".

First, God is Accomplishing His Original Plan in Us.

God's original plan for man was a righteous relationship with Him. That relationship was interrupted by sin.

Secondly, God is Building Our Patience (**verse 3**).

He allows our trials to build our ability to wait with earnest expectation that the hope within us will be fulfilled. **(Psalms 27:14; Isaiah 40:31; Romans 5:3)**

Thirdly, He teaches us how to be mature Christians (**verse 4**).

God's ultimate goal for man was to build a creature that is complete in His relationship with His Creator. Creatures that could choose to love Him, choose to love those around them, and choose to love themselves – No Matter What! **(St. Matthew 5:48)**

Summary:

Your purpose is bigger than you and only God can safely lead you to that place in Him. In order to walk into the Commanded Blessing for your life, you must endure the preliminary trials. “The Trials that Unveil your Purpose”!

Lesson 9:

Acceptable and Perfect Will of God!!!

Definition: Perfect – that which has reached its end; no more to complete.

The theme in the book of **Romans** is the revelation of God's wrath against sin. It also unveil that righteousness through faith is the grounds of justification. This book contains the fundamentals of Christian education. It shows that the whole world is guilty before God and in need of salvation through our Lord and Savior Jesus Christ. People are now to bring themselves as a living sacrifice to God instead of bringing animals as sacrifices as in the days of old. As we completely yield ourselves to God, we discover six things that constitute the acceptable and perfect will of God:

I. Present our bodies a living sacrifice to God **(Rom. 1:5; Eph. 3:8).**

II. Make the body holy. **(Rom. 12:1; II Cor. 7:1)**

III. Make self-acceptable to God. **(Rom. 12:1)**

IV. Render reasonable service. **(Rom. 12:1)**

V. Be not conformed to the world. **(Rom. 12:2)**

VI. Be transformed from the world. **(Rom. 12:2)**

Summary:

The acceptable and perfect will of God includes the total yielding of the individual to God. There is no holding back on our part. We let go of any and all things that are a potential hindrance to a healthy and unspotted relationship with God.

Lesson 10:

The Otherness of God!!!

Scripture Text:
Deuteronomy 5:6-12; II Cor. 4:18

Definition: Otherness– the quality or state of being different or distinct in appearance, character, etc.

No doubt; when you think of God there are certain words that come to mind. We are aware of God's Omniscience, Omnipotence, Omnipresence and Immutability. We are aware of His Righteousness, Justice and Holiness. Yet there remains a part of God that we can only speculate. We will call this **the Otherness of God**.

Let us examine closer this incapable of knowing yet obvious part of our Great Big God:

I. God loves mankind but we can't understand His kind of love. **(John 3:16)**

II. We don't always understand the timing of God, He's never too late. **(Ps. 46:1)**

III. We so many times miss the signs of His presence in our affairs. **(Acts 17:28)**

IV. We can't logically discern His Will during our troubled times.**(II Cor. 4:8)**

V. Of all mankind, we don't know why He chose us as His vessels. **(II Cor. 4:7)**

VI. Why were we made as free moral agents? **(Psalms 139:14)**

VII. In judgment of our wrongs He's yet merciful. **(Genesis 3:15)**

VIII. His longsuffering is immeasurable. **(Exodus 34:6)**

IX. His loving-kindness is convicting and drawing. **(Jeremiah 31:3)**

X. In His hiddenness He's yet visible. **(Isaiah 45:15)**

XI. His thoughts and plans for us are overwhelming. **(Jeremiah 29:11)**

XII. Angels worship Him to the third degree crying: **1**.holy, **2**.holy, **3**.holy **(Isa. 6:3)**

Summary:

The Otherness of God encapsulates everything about God that we don't know. Even those things about God we think we know are too vast for our finite minds to contain. In the grandeur of His being, God has robed Himself in awesomeness. It is to our benefit to seek Him diligently without wavering and without being distracted by the cares of this short life we are living.

About the Author

Bishop Ronnie Whittier lives in St. Louis, Missouri where he serves as Senior Pastor of Emmanuel Temple Church of God. He is co-founder of Resurrection of Christ Fellowship Church located in Guyana, South America. In addition, he has travelled extensively to various countries sharing the Gospel. He is married to his beautiful wife, Lady Winnetta L. Whittier and has three lovely and gifted daughters, Keisha, Alexis, and Rhonda.

www.ingramcontent.com/pod-product-compliance
Lightning Source LLC
Chambersburg PA
CBHW071956040426
42447CB00009B/1364

* 9 7 8 0 5 7 8 4 6 7 7 9 5 *